APPLE WATCH SERIES 8 SENIORS GUIDE

Unlock the Full Potential of Your Apple Watch and Revolutionize Your Digital Lifestyle and Well-Being

John Halbert

TABLE OF CONTENTS

INTRODUCTION

The Apple Watch has revolutionized the way we interact with technology and manage our daily lives. Since its introduction in 2015, it has become one of the most popular smartwatches on the market, with its intuitive user interface, health and fitness tracking capabilities, and seamless integration with other Apple devices.

With each new iteration, the Apple Watch adds powerful features to help users stay connected, active and informed. The recently released Apple Watch Series 8 takes this to the next level with sophisticated sensors to provide deeper health insights, improved safety features for better protection, and excellent customizability for a personalized experience.

For senior users, the Apple Watch offers a multitude of benefits that can enrich their daily lives. It promotes an active lifestyle to support healthy aging, enables convenient communication with loved ones, and enhances independence and safety. However, the complexity of smartwatches can also be daunting for those unfamiliar or uncomfortable with modern technology.

This comprehensive guide aims to make the Apple Watch Series 8 accessible for senior users. It explores how to optimize Apple Watch setup, customize preferences for the comfort of use, and navigate key features through simple, step-by-step instructions. With an intuitive, user-friendly approach, this book helps seniors fully harness the Apple Watch's capabilities for maximum impact on their well-being.

We begin with an overview of Apple Watch basics, including how to interact with the display using the Digital Crown, side button, and taps and presses on the screen. Readers learn core operations like accessing apps, managing notifications, understanding icons and symbols, and more. Guidance is provided on setup options to simplify the interface, such as decreasing icon numbers, increasing text size, and adjusting brightness and font size for optimal viewing.

Next, the book dives into customizing the Apple Watch to suit seniors' needs and preferences. Directions are provided on selecting watch face styles, modifying complications to display desired information, rearranging apps in the dock, and adjusting sounds and haptic feedback for notifications. Readers also learn how to utilize the many accessibility features built into watchOS to support impaired vision, hearing, motor skills, and more.

Mastering key features like Siri, Messages, and Phone is essential for staying connected on the Apple Watch, so we explore voice commands, dictation, reading and replying to messages, making and answering calls directly on the watch, and other communication options. The Family Setup feature is explained for sharing an Apple Watch with family members who don't have an iPhone.

A major appeal of the Apple Watch for seniors is the focus on health, fitness, and safety. This book offers guidance on heart rate monitoring, ECG and blood oxygen apps, fall detection and Emergency SOS, sleep and environmental sound tracking for better rest, personalized Move goals with activity reminders, wheelchair pace and push tracking, and much more. By understanding these health metrics and alerts, seniors can optimize their well-being.

Beyond health tools, we explore convenient everyday apps like Calendar, Reminders, Timers, News, Find My Watch, and Wallet. Useful settings like theater mode, water lock, and power reserve are covered to help seniors use the watch comfortably in different environments. Advanced features like Apple Pay, walkie-talkie, and third-party apps are also introduced for seniors who want to extend the functionality of their Apple Watch.

Throughout the book, tips are provided to troubleshoot common issues, maximize battery life, boost security and privacy, and seamlessly integrate the Apple Watch into daily routines. For seniors looking to enrich their lives through wearable technology, this guide unlocks the full potential of the Apple Watch Series 8. Let's get started on your journey towards better health, connectivity, and independence!

CHAPTER 1

APPLE WATCH SERIES 8 BASICS

Navigating the Watch

With its intuitive controls, health and safety features, and deep iPhone integration, the Apple Watch has become a popular device for tech-savvy seniors looking to stay active and connected. The latest Apple Watch Series 8 takes these capabilities even further.

But for first-time Apple Watch owners, learning to navigate the watch and access key features can be daunting. This section will walk you through the core aspects of using your Apple Watch Series 8, from the basics of swiping and scrolling to customizing your watch face to using must-have apps and tools. Follow along to get up and running with your new wearable companion.

Getting Started: Controls and Navigation

If you're new to smartwatches, the first step is understanding how to move around and interact with your Apple Watch. While it may take some practice at first, the navigation will soon feel natural and intuitive.

When you first lift your wrist or tap the screen, you'll see your watch face with apps laid out around it. The watch face shows core info like the time, date, weather, and activity rings. You can customize it later.

1. To open an app, just tap its icon.
2. To return to the watch face from any screen, press the Digital Crown button on the right side of the watch.

The Digital Crown is your primary tool for navigation.

1. Turn it to scroll down lists or zoom in and out of maps.
2. Press it to return home.
3. The Crown also brings up Siri if you hold it down to activate voice commands.

You can also swipe side to side and up and down directly on the touchscreen. Swipe left and right to switch between widgets like weather forecasts or calendar events. Swipe down from the top edge to access notifications. Try both scrolling the Digital Crown and swiping the touchscreen to see which you prefer for navigation. With practice, this will start to feel very natural.

Customizing Your Watch Face

One of the joys of the Apple Watch is customizing your watch face to suit your tastes and needs through different designs, colors, and complications.

1. Swipe left or right across your current watch face to browse designs.
2. Tap the one you like to switch your watch face.
3. You can also long-press the face, then tap Edit or Customize to change design elements.

In the Face Gallery, tap New at the bottom to browse additional watch faces.

1. Select one you like to add. Some faces, like Photos or Motion, allow you to set a background photo from your library or a dynamic motion pattern.
2. Try several on to see your favorite aesthetic.

You can also tweak which complications appear on your watch face for at-a-glance info. Complications include info like weather, activity rings, battery level, or upcoming calendar events.

Long press the watch face again, tap Edit Complications, then tap on a complication to change what it displays. For example, change the bottom left to show your next appointment instead of the date. Take time to play around with watch faces and complications to create the perfect customized watch face.

Mastering Key Apps and Features

Now that you're comfortable with general navigation, it's time to dive into apps and features that make the Apple Watch so powerful for seniors. These tools can enrich your day-to-day life and give you confidence on the go.

Health and Activity Tracking

One of the most useful functions of the Apple Watch for seniors is health and fitness tracking.

1. Swipe up from the bottom of the watch face to open the Control Center.
2. Here, you'll find your Activity rings showing Move, Exercise and Stand progress.
3. Tap each one to see specific stats for that day.

You can also view more detailed tracking data by opening the Activity app. Swipe left to check daily habits like steps taken, distance covered, minutes active, and hourly movement. This helps encourage staying active each day.

An important safety feature for seniors is Fall Detection. Go to the Apple Watch app on your iPhone and enable Fall Detection so the watch can alert emergency services if it senses you've taken a hard fall.

Heart Health Monitoring

The Apple Watch Series 8 has sensors that can take an ECG reading to check for irregular heart rhythms like atrial fibrillation.

1. To take an ECG, open the ECG app.
2. Rest your finger on the Digital Crown and hold still for 30 seconds as the watch takes the reading.

You can view and share ECG results with your doctor via the Health app on your iPhone. This makes proactive heart health monitoring easy.

Emergency SOS

For worst-case scenarios, Emergency SOS can provide a lifeline.

- Press and hold the side button on your Apple Watch to place a call to emergency services and designated emergency contacts.

To set up Emergency Contacts, open the Apple Watch app on your iPhone and go to Emergency SOS. Add contact names so the watch can notify loved ones if you need help.

Walkie-Talkie and Find My Apps

Two other apps that make connecting easy are Walkie-Talkie and Find My. Open Walkie-Talkie and select a friend who has an Apple Watch to do voice chats back and forth with just a button press.

If you misplace your iPhone, use Find My right from your watch to make your phone ring loudly to locate it. Just open the Find My app and tap your device name to ping it.

Staying Connected Through Messages, Mail and Calls

Messaging from your watch makes staying in touch convenient. When a text or iMessage comes in, swipe down from the top of your watch face to read it. You can send quick preset replies like "OK" or dictate responses via dictation or Siri. For emails, the Mail app lets you read, reply to, flag, and archive messages straight from your wrist. Scroll through with the Digital Crown to navigate long emails. To make calls, you can speak to Siri or navigate to the Phone app. Scroll to choose a favorite contact to call and raise your wrist to speak. To answer calls, just tap the green Accept button.

Essential Settings to Customize

Don't forget to poke around in Settings on your watch to personalize and optimize the experience. Swipe up from the bottom of your watch face to find Settings. Under Sounds & Haptics, make sure the volume and alerts are loud enough. Toggle Prominent Haptic on for stronger vibrations.

In Display, you can increase text size or enable Zoom to make content easier to see. Turn on the Wake Screen and make sure Raise to Wake is on to activate the screen without tapping.

Lastly, enable Theater Mode if you want the screen to stay dark and mute alerts when in shows or churches. Toggle this handy setting in the Control Center.

Final Words

Learning to navigate your Apple Watch opens up a world of convenient connections, health insights, safety features, and more right from your wrist. Take time to explore all the watch has to offer and customize the settings for your needs. Soon, wearing your Apple Watch daily will become second nature, keeping you active, informed, and engaged wherever you go.

Customizing Settings

One of the best features of the Apple Watch is its vast array of personalization options and settings to customize the device specifically for senior users. With the Watch's latest Series 8 model, there are more ways than ever to tweak the watch to best fit your lifestyle, needs, and preferences.

In this section, we'll explore key settings seniors should know to tailor their Apple Watch experience. From crafting your ideal watch face to configuring notifications, accessibility, sounds, apps and more, these tips will help you optimize your Apple Watch to be your perfect wearable companion.

Crafting the Ideal Watch Face

The watch face is your home base—the screen that greets you whenever you raise your wrist or tap the display. Apple makes it easy to customize your watch face to suit your tastes.

Swipe left or right across the current watch face to browse and switch between designs. Tap Customize or Edit to change design elements. You can also add or remove complications, which are the handy snippets of info that appear around the watch face periphery.

Some face favorites for seniors include:

- Photo face: Show off treasured family pics and memories.
- Analog or digital faces: Choose classic and clear time displays.

- The utility faces like Infograph Modular or California: Pack in useful complications like weather, calendar, activity rings, or battery level.
- Solar Dial or Astronomy: Fun scientific faces with solar or lunar themes.

Don't hesitate to get creative and regularly change up your watch face! It's an easy way to refresh your watch.

Optimizing Notifications

Controlling notifications is key, so you only receive alerts that are relevant. Too many pings can become aggravating.

1. On your iPhone's Apple Watch app, tap Notifications to review which apps send alerts.
2. Tap an app and select Custom to set specific alerts. For example, limit phone calls and texts to mirror your iPhone while disabling email notifications.
3. In watch Settings, go to Notifications > Scheduled Summary to bundle non-time-sensitive alerts for periodic delivery like every morning and evening rather than constant pestering.

Adjust Text Size for Easy Reading

Apple Watch allows you to enlarge text for improved readability.

Under Settings > Display & Brightness, toggle Bold Text on. Also, adjust Text Size to see what's most comfortable for you.

You can also enable Zoom, found under General > Accessibility. Triple-click the Digital Crown button to zoom in on the whole screen. This helps highlight buttons and details.

Add Prominent Haptic Feedback

The Apple Watch uses subtle haptic pulses to tap your wrist for alerts. For stronger feedback, toggle Prominent Haptics on under Sound & Haptics settings. This helps ensure you don't miss notifications.

Boost Alert Volume

While Apple Watch speakers work well for calls and Siri, you may need a louder volume for alerts.

1. In Sounds & Haptics settings, drag the volume slider toward the max volume.
2. Toggle Change with Buttons off so volume buttons don't affect alerts.

Magnify Feature Actions

Under Accessibility settings, there's a useful option called Magnifier. When triple-clicked, this acts like a magnifying glass to enlarge button names and text you touch for precise control.

Enable Fall Detection

A must-have safety feature for seniors is Fall Detection, found in Emergency SOS settings. This uses motion sensors to detect if you've taken a hard fall and remained motionless, then calls emergency services on your behalf. Provide emergency contacts, too, for additional alerts.

Customize Side Button

The side button below the Digital Crown can be set to your preferred function. Try changing it to open Apple Pay or launch Walkie-Talkie for quick access instead of the default Siri function.

Streamline Frequently Used Apps

To surface your favorite apps, open the Watch app on your iPhone and tap Dock. Drag your most-used apps like Phone, Messages, Reminders, Weather and Wallet into the dock for quick access from your watch face.

Set a Bedtime Schedule

The Wind Down feature helps the Apple Watch nudge you toward sleep by quieting and dimming the display at a chosen bedtime. Try this under General > Bedtime to maintain better sleep habits and reduce disruptive late-night alerts.

Activate Theater Mode

Heading to the movies or a show? Swipe up for Control Center on your watch and tap the drama masks icon to enable Theater Mode. This mutes audio alerts and dims the screen to avoid disturbance while maintaining time visibility.

Personalize Watch Faces for Different Times of Day

Create custom watch faces suited for daytime, evening, sleeping, and working out. Swipe to each one at appropriate times for a tailored experience all day long. Tap the X to delete less-used faces.

For at-a-glance visibility into remaining battery life, add the battery complication. Tap and hold your watch face, tap Edit Complications, then choose Battery Percentage or Battery Level for the rundown at all times.

Add Meaningful Contextual Info

Complications aren't limited to just battery or calendar. Tap and hold the watch face again, then edit complications to display useful details like activity ring progress, next appointment, stock quotes, world clocks showing different time zones, weather forecasts, or moon phases. Try mixes to find your ideal layout.

Turn on AssistiveTouch

AssistiveTouch under Accessibility provides an onscreen home button if the physical side button is difficult to press. Customize gestures to perform actions like taking a screenshot, waking the display, or opening the Control Center through taps instead.

Activate the Wake Screen on the Wrist Raise

Under General settings, ensure Raise to Wake is enabled so that simply lifting and turning your wrist wakes your Apple Watch display automatically without needing to tap. This makes using the watch seamless.

As you can see, the options for customizing the Apple Watch are incredibly deep. Spend time tailoring these settings to craft your perfect experience. Once set up, your Apple Watch will feel like an invaluable personal assistant. Enjoy!

Interacting with Siri

One of the most helpful features of the Apple Watch for seniors is the ability to use Siri, Apple's intelligent voice assistant. With just your voice, you can send messages, set timers and alarms, track information, and much more.

The latest Apple Watch Series 8 integrates Siri even more seamlessly into the experience through new natural language interactions and expanded capabilities. In this section, we'll go through all the ways seniors can get the most out of Siri on their Apple Watch to simplify and enhance daily life.

Activating Siri on Your Apple Watch

The first step is knowing all the ways you can summon Siri to assist you on your Apple Watch. Siri is activated hands-free to allow convenience and ease of use.

The main method is to press and hold the Digital Crown on the side of the watch until you see the Siri waveform animation and hear the Siri tone. After the tone, speak your request clearly.

You can also just raise your wrist and say "Hey Siri" to activate the assistant without pressing anything. Make sure Raise to Speak is enabled in Settings > Siri so your watch listens for the "Hey Siri" cue.

For quick Siri access, double press the side button to instantly get Siri's attention. Triple-press the side button if you have mobility limitations for even faster Siri activation.

Once Siri is listening, speak in clear, natural language. You don't need overly complex commands. Simple phrasing like "Set a timer for 10 minutes" or "Text my daughter I'm on my way" works great.

Useful Tips for Interacting with Siri

Here are some useful tips to get the most out of talking with Siri on your Apple Watch:

- Wait until you see the Siri waveform or hear the chime sound before speaking. This ensures Siri is actively listening.

- Speak at a natural volume and pace, enunciating words clearly. There's no need to yell.
- Give Siri one task at a time, like "Tell me the weather forecast today in Houston." Don't overload it with multiple requests at once.
- If Siri gets the request wrong, you can say "Cancel" to start over or try rephrasing more clearly.
- To have Siri read long responses out loud, say, "Hey Siri, read that." This is helpful without having to view the small screen.
- Personalize commands using relationships and locations. Try "Call my grandson Alex" or "Find coffee shops near me."
- Summon Siri from any screen. You don't have to be on the watch face. The assistant pops up, ready to help.

Must-Use Siri Commands for Seniors

Siri's capabilities on the Apple Watch seem almost endless. But these are some of the most useful commands seniors should know to take advantage of Siri every day:

- Set timers and alarms ("Set a 20-minute timer for the casserole" or "Set an alarm for 7 am tomorrow")
- Get information ("How's the weather today?" or "What's on my calendar for this afternoon?")
- Send messages and emails ("Text my wife that I'll be home soon" or "Email Tom about dinner tonight")
- Place calls ("Call my doctor" or "Call Alice on speakerphone")
- Control music and podcasts ("Play some jazz music" or "Skip this song")
- Launch apps ("Open Transit" or "Launch the Reminders app")
- Capture photos ("Take a picture" or "Take a selfie")
- Adjust settings ("Turn on theater mode" or "Set volume to 50%")
- Start workouts ("Start an outdoor walk" or "Begin a cardio workout")
- Get directions and traffic info ("Give me directions home avoiding highways" or "How's traffic to the airport?")
- Check stocks, weather, calendar, and news ("How is the Dow Jones today?" "What's the weather this weekend?" "When is my dentist appointment?" "Read my news briefing")

As you can see, Siri allows you to access almost everything on your Apple Watch using just the sound of your voice. Keep exploring new ways Siri can help simplify your interactions.

Optimizing Siri for Your Needs

Don't forget you can customize Siri to better fit your preferences under Apple Watch Settings > Siri.

1. Turn on or off Raise to Speak and Hey Siri functionality.
2. Select your preferred Siri voice and language. Automatically have Siri read responses to you for convenience.
3. Enable Siri complications for quick access to common Siri tasks right from your watch face.

You can also allow Siri access to your personal data like calendars, contacts, health information, and more for more personalized assistance. However, limit access if you have privacy concerns surrounding your information.

In Settings > Siri & Search, you can opt to have Siri help find content on your watch and suggest actions based on your daily patterns. This provides helpful recommendations over time.

Lastly, under Accessibility settings, switch on Hold to Speak if you'd like to manually activate Siri by holding the Digital Crown before speaking. And toggle Tap to Speak to summon Siri by double tapping instead of voice. Customize to what works for you!

The Takeaway on Siri for Seniors

Siri is an invaluable resource for Apple Watch users thanks to its hands-free convenience and wide range of capabilities. Take time to consistently practice talking to Siri and customizing the settings to best meet your needs.

Soon, your Apple Watch and the powerful Siri assistant will feel like your personalized helper, making daily tasks, communication, information gathering and more frictionless. You'll wonder how you ever managed without it! With Siri at your beck and call, your Apple Watch becomes an extension of you.

CHAPTER 2

HEALTH AND WELLNESS FEATURES

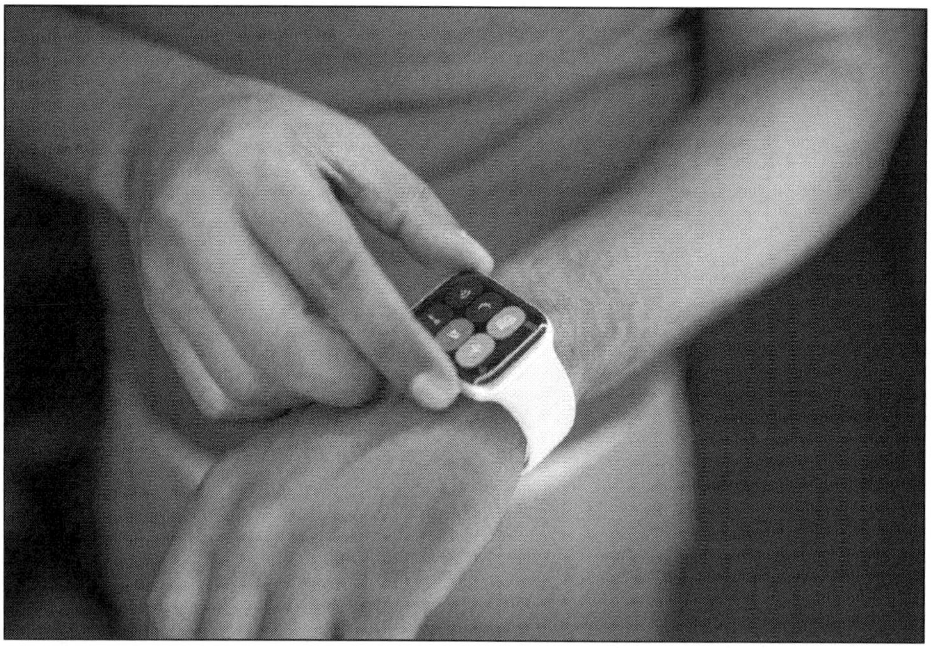

Monitoring Heart Rate

One of the most significant health features of the Apple Watch for older adults is the ability to passively monitor your heart rate throughout the day and during workouts. The Apple Watch Series 8 takes this even further with next-level heart rate tracking capabilities and alerts.

For seniors, keeping an eye on your heart rate provides vital insight into overall cardiovascular health and can reveal early signs of potential issues like arrhythmias. In this chapter, we'll explore how seniors can utilize the Apple Watch's extensive heart rate toolkit for proactive health.

Understanding Resting, Active, and Recovery Heart Rate

The Apple Watch uses its electrical heart rate sensor and accelerometer to track heart rate all day and night. But what do all the numbers mean?

Your resting heart rate is your pulse when relaxed and inactive. For most people, a normal range is 60 to 100 BPM. Higher resting heart rates may indicate developing health problems. When you exercise, your heart rate increases in response to exertion. This is your active heart rate. Harder workouts drive your heart rate higher into cardio and peak zones.

Recovery heart rate is how quickly your pulse returns to normal after exercise. Fitter individuals recover faster. Slow recovery could signal health issues like heart disease. The Apple Watch records all these heart rate zones and patterns to establish your baseline. Deviations can provide early health alerts.

How to View Your Heart Rate Data

The Apple Watch makes heart rate data easy to access. Simply swipe up from the bottom of the watch face to reveal the Control Center. Your current heart rate in BPM will display.

For historical data, open the Heart Rate app on your watch. You'll see graphs of your heart rate throughout the day, along with average and high/low readings. Swipe left through different days.

In the Health app on your paired iPhone, you can also view heart rate data like resting rate, walking average, cardio training average, and recovery rates after workouts.

Enabling High and Low Heart Rate Alerts

A helpful way the Apple Watch monitors your heart health is through high heart rate and low heart rate notifications. If your heart rate spikes abnormally high when inactive, it could signal issues like infection or atrial fibrillation. Low heart rate alerts may catch problems like bradycardia.

- To enable the alerts, open the Watch app and go to Heart > High Heart Rate and Low Heart Rate.

Adjust the BPM threshold and choose whether to get notified. When your heart rate sustains over or under the set threshold, even when still, your Apple Watch will notify you so you can consult a doctor if it recurs.

Tracking Your Heart Rate During Exercise

When you record a workout on your Apple Watch, either through the Workout app or third-party apps like Strava, the watch tracks your live heart rate throughout. You'll see current, average, and max heart rates displayed on the workout metric screens in real time so you can monitor exertion. Heart rate zones like cardio and peak will also show during intense workouts.

After your workout concludes, you get a detailed heart rate graph in the Fitness app on your iPhone showing the peaks, valleys, averages and how your heart rate varied during the full session.

This data can help optimize your training and make sure you're hitting target heart rate zones for your age and fitness level during exercise.

Getting Alerted for Irregular Rhythms

Significant heart rate alerts on Apple Watch go beyond just high or low readings. With the ECG app, the watch can notify you if it detects potential atrial fibrillation (AFib). AFib is an irregular heart rhythm that leads to complications like stroke and heart failure. By getting notified when the watch detects signs of AFib, you can proactively see a doctor and treat it earlier. To enable AFib notifications, install the ECG app on your Apple Watch if you haven't already and enable Irregular Rhythm Notifications. Be sure to review any prompts or results with your physician.

How Heart Rate Factors into Calories Burned

When tracking activity and exercise with the Apple Watch, you may be wondering how heart rate impacts estimated calorie burn. The watch factors your personal heart rate data into its calorie formula along with inputs like your height, weight, age, and type of movement.

Higher heart rates during intense exercise result in more calories burned than lower-heart-rate activities like walking. But any movement helps drive up the heart rate to burn additional calories.

Enabling Heart Rate Complications and Watch Faces

For at-a-glance visibility into your current heart rate throughout the day, add heart rate complications to your Apple Watch faces.

Customize your chosen watch face by long pressing the display, then selecting heart rate data to see as complications. Choices include:

- Heart Rate - Shows your live BPM in a numerical complication.
- Heart Rate Graph - Displays a tiny line graph of your heart rate that updates.
- Breath - Animates a breath graphic based on your pulse.

There are also dedicated heart rate watch faces like Kaleidoscope, which dynamically displays your heart rate in a mesmerizing pattern. Browse the watch face gallery for other heart rate-focused options.

Tracking Physical Activity

Physical activity is the cornerstone of a healthy and fulfilling life, regardless of age. As we gracefully age, the importance of maintaining an active lifestyle becomes paramount. The Apple Watch Series 8, with its cutting-edge technology and health-centric features, stands as a guiding companion for seniors keen on tracking and enhancing their physical activities. In this section, we will delve deeper into the myriad ways this smartwatch effectively tracks physical activity, motivating and aiding seniors in achieving their health and fitness goals.

Understanding Physical Activity Tracking

Physical activity tracking, facilitated by the Apple Watch Series 8, involves monitoring various movements and exercises performed throughout the day. This encompasses activities like walking, running, cycling, swimming, yoga, and more. The watch employs an amalgamation of sensors, including an accelerometer, gyroscope, and GPS, to detect and measure these movements accurately.

Accelerometer

The accelerometer in the Apple Watch detects changes in motion and measures the acceleration of your body. It determines the number of steps you take, your pace, and the intensity of your movements, providing a fundamental basis for tracking physical activity.

Gyroscope

Complementing the accelerometer, the gyroscope measures the orientation and rotation of your wrist. This is particularly useful for activities like cycling or weightlifting, where the movement might not involve typical steps but still contribute to your overall physical activity.

GPS

For outdoor activities like running or cycling, the built-in GPS in the Apple Watch Series 8 accurately tracks your route, distance covered, and elevation. This enhances the precision of the data recorded and offers a more comprehensive view of your outdoor physical activities.

Comprehensive Physical Activity Monitoring

The Apple Watch Series 8 offers a comprehensive approach to physical activity monitoring, catering to a wide range of exercises and daily movements. Seniors can choose from various workout types preloaded on the watch, including but not limited to:

Walking

Walking is a low-impact exercise that many seniors find suitable for maintaining their fitness. The Apple Watch accurately tracks the duration, distance, pace, and heart rate during walks, providing a holistic view of your walking routine. Whether it's a leisurely stroll in the park or a brisk walk for cardiovascular benefits, the watch helps you stay on track.

Running

For seniors who enjoy running, the Apple Watch Series 8 becomes an indispensable tool. It monitors your pace, distance, and heart rate and even provides insights into your running form. By analyzing this data, you can make adjustments to your running style and optimize your performance while minimizing the risk of injury.

Cycling

Cycling is a fantastic, low-impact exercise that is gentle on the joints. The Apple Watch accurately tracks your cycling routes using GPS and measures your speed, distance, and heart rate. This information aids in setting achievable cycling goals and improving your cardiovascular health.

Swimming

Swimming is an excellent full-body workout, and the Apple Watch Series 8 is water-resistant, making it ideal for tracking your swimming sessions. The watch can monitor your laps, stroke style, distance, and calories burned while swimming. This comprehensive data helps you fine-tune your swimming technique and enhance your overall fitness.

Yoga

Yoga is a popular choice among seniors for its gentle yet effective approach to fitness. The Apple Watch offers a yoga workout option that tracks your heart rate, duration, and calories burned during your yoga sessions. This feature encourages regular yoga practice and allows you to measure your progress over time.

Strength Training

Strength training is essential for seniors to maintain muscle mass and bone density. While it may not involve extensive movement, the Apple Watch Series 8 uses its sensors to detect and record your movements during strength training exercises. Tracking your heart rate and effort during strength workouts helps you tailor your routines for maximum benefit.

Setting Goals and Achievements

One of the remarkable aspects of the Apple Watch Series 8 is its ability to set personalized physical activity goals based on your age, weight, and activity level. These goals are intelligently designed to encourage consistent effort and gradual progress. Seniors can customize their daily goals, such as the number of calories to burn, the duration of exercise, or the number of steps to take, aligning with their capabilities and aspirations.

As you achieve these goals, the watch rewards you with badges and achievements, fostering a sense of accomplishment and motivating you to maintain an active lifestyle. The sense of achievement encourages seniors to challenge themselves further, leading to improved fitness levels and an enhanced quality of life.

Real-Time Monitoring and Feedback

The Apple Watch Series 8 provides real-time feedback during your workouts, offering a wealth of information at a glance. As you engage in physical activities, you can easily view essential metrics such as heart rate, duration, distance, and calories burned directly on the watch's display. This immediate feedback allows seniors to make necessary adjustments to their intensity or pace during the workout, ensuring a safe and effective exercise routine.

Furthermore, the watch utilizes haptic feedback, providing subtle vibrations for milestones achieved, encouraging you to persevere and reach your set goals. This tactile feedback is gentle and unobtrusive, making the overall tracking experience more engaging and interactive.

Sleep Tracking for Enhanced Wellness

In addition to tracking your daytime physical activities, the Apple Watch Series 8 also incorporates advanced sleep-tracking features. Adequate sleep is crucial for overall well-being, and the watch monitors your sleep patterns, duration, and quality to provide insights into your sleep hygiene. This holistic approach to health encompasses not only being active during the day but also ensuring restorative sleep at night, which is particularly vital for seniors.

The Apple Watch Series 8 is a revolutionary tool that has redefined how seniors approach physical activity and overall wellness. Through its precise tracking capabilities, personalized goal setting, and real-time feedback, seniors are empowered to embrace an active lifestyle. By engaging in regular physical activity and utilizing the myriad features of the Apple Watch Series 8, seniors can proactively enhance their physical fitness, emotional well-being, and overall quality of life. This smartwatch serves as an encouraging companion on the path to a healthier and happier future, exemplifying the marriage of technology and health for the benefit of seniors and individuals of all ages.

Managing Health Data

Health data management is a crucial aspect of contemporary healthcare, especially with the rapid integration of technology into our daily lives. The Apple Watch Series 8 offers a comprehensive and intuitive approach to managing health data, allowing users to monitor, organize, and analyze their health-related information efficiently. In this section, we will delve into the various aspects of managing health data with the Apple Watch Series 8 and how it aids in promoting proactive health management, particularly for seniors.

The Health App: A Centralized Hub

At the core of health data management on the Apple Watch Series 8 is the Health app. This app serves as a centralized hub for all health and wellness-related information collected by the watch and other compatible health and fitness apps. It acts as a repository that accumulates a wide array of data, including heart rate, physical activity, sleep patterns, nutrition, medications, and more.

The Health app offers a user-friendly interface that allows seniors to view their health data in a clear and organized manner. The data is presented through easy-to-read graphs, charts, and summaries, enabling users to track their progress over time. This visual representation of health data is particularly beneficial for seniors, making it easier for them to comprehend and interpret their health metrics.

Moreover, the Health app categorizes health data into different sections, making it simple to navigate and locate specific information. Seniors can easily access their vital signs, such as heart rate and blood pressure, physical activity metrics, mindfulness data, nutrition details, and more, all within a few taps on their paired iPhone.

Integration and Synchronization

One of the standout advantages of the Apple Watch Series 8 is its seamless integration and synchronization with the Health app on the paired iPhone. The watch continuously collects health data throughout the day, including heart rate, steps, distance, and even the duration and quality of sleep. This data is then automatically and securely synchronized with the Health app whenever the watch is connected to the iPhone.

The integration and synchronization process ensure that seniors have access to real-time health data on their iPhones, providing a comprehensive view of their overall health and wellness. The information gathered by the watch is not only useful for personal tracking but can also be shared with healthcare professionals during medical consultations, enabling more informed discussions and decision-making.

This app allows for data sharing with other compatible health and fitness apps, creating a comprehensive health ecosystem. Seniors can choose to integrate data from third-party apps, such as nutrition trackers or specialized exercise apps, into the Health app, providing a holistic view of their health journey.

Privacy and Security

Given the sensitive nature of health data, privacy and security are paramount concerns. Apple recognizes this and has implemented robust measures to ensure the confidentiality and security of health information stored on the Apple Watch Series 8 and within the Health app.

All health data collected and stored on the Apple Watch Series 8 and synchronized with the Health app is encrypted, ensuring that only authorized users can access and view it. The data is protected by advanced security features, including biometric authentication (such as Touch ID or Face ID) and passcodes, adding an extra layer of protection.

Moreover, Apple has designed the Health app to give users control over their data. Seniors can choose what information they want to share and with whom. Whether it's granting access to specific health professionals or sharing data with a family member, the user retains control and can tailor the level of access as needed.

Customization and Goal Setting

A notable feature of the Health app is its ability to facilitate customization and goal setting. Seniors can set personalized health goals based on their unique needs, preferences, and recommendations from healthcare professionals. Whether the goal is to increase daily step count, lower resting heart rate, or improve sleep duration, the app provides a platform to establish achievable targets.

As seniors progress towards their set goals, the app tracks their performance and provides regular updates on their achievements. This aspect of gamification motivates and encourages seniors to stay committed to their health objectives. The sense of accomplishment derived from reaching milestones further fuels their dedication to maintaining a healthy and active lifestyle.

Additionally, the Health app offers a "Trends" feature that showcases long-term progress, allowing seniors to identify patterns and make informed adjustments to their health routines. This analytical feature assists in refining goals and optimizing health strategies for better outcomes.

Empowering Better Healthcare Decisions

By effectively managing their health data through the Apple Watch Series 8 and the Health app, seniors are empowered to make better healthcare decisions. The availability of comprehensive and up-to-date health information allows for a more accurate assessment of their well-being and provides valuable insights into their overall health trends.

Seniors can proactively share their health data with their healthcare providers during medical consultations. This data-driven approach facilitates more informed discussions, accurate diagnoses, and personalized treatment plans. It streamlines the communication between seniors and their healthcare team, promoting a collaborative approach to healthcare management.

The ability to track various health metrics over time enables seniors to identify potential health issues early. Whether it's noticing a sudden increase in resting heart rate or irregular sleep patterns, the Apple Watch Series 8 serves as an early warning system, prompting seniors to seek medical attention promptly and potentially preventing more severe health complications.

The Apple Watch Series 8, coupled with the Health app, has redefined the way we manage and utilize health data. For seniors, this powerful combination offers an opportunity to take control of their health and wellness journey like never before. The centralized hub of the Health app, seamless integration and synchronization, privacy and security measures, customization and goal setting, and the ability to make informed decisions empower seniors to lead healthier lives.

As we continue to embrace technology in healthcare, the Apple Watch Series 8 stands as a testament to the potential of wearable devices to revolutionize proactive health management, especially for the senior population. By leveraging the features and capabilities of this smartwatch, seniors can navigate their health with confidence, knowledge, and a newfound sense of empowerment.

CHAPTER 3

STAYING CONNECTED

The Apple Watch Series 8 has evolved into a powerful companion for seniors, offering a range of features designed to keep them connected and secure. In this chapter, we will delve into the essentials of staying connected with the Apple Watch Series 8, focusing on making and receiving calls, sending messages, and utilizing the Emergency SOS feature. We'll provide step-by-step instructions to ensure seniors can effectively use these functions and make the most out of their Apple Watch experience.

Making and Receiving Calls

Making and receiving calls on the Apple Watch Series 8 is a seamless and convenient experience, providing seniors with a direct line of communication right on their wrist. This feature ensures they stay connected with loved ones, healthcare providers, or emergency services at all times. In this section, we will take an in-depth look at how to make and receive calls step by step on the Apple Watch Series 8.

Initiating a Call

To initiate a call, start by waking up your Apple Watch Series 8. You can do this by raising your wrist or tapping the screen. The watch face will light up, displaying the time and any complications you have set. If you have enabled Always On Display, you will be able to see this information without any interaction.

Now, locate and tap the Phone app icon, which is represented by a green phone receiver. The Phone app is typically located on the home screen or in the app layout, easily accessible with a tap. Once you've tapped the Phone app, the watch will take you to the Phone interface.

In the Phone interface, you will see a '+' button. Tapping this button allows you to access your contacts. The Apple Watch Series 8 syncs with your iPhone's contacts, providing you with a list of your saved contacts. Alternatively, you can use Siri, Apple's virtual assistant, by saying, "Hey Siri, call [contact name]." Siri will process your request and initiate the call.

Choose the desired contact from your list or the one suggested by Siri. Tap the contact's name to start the call. The Apple Watch Series 8 will then connect the call, and you'll be able to converse with the recipient.

Receiving a Call

When you receive an incoming call on your paired iPhone, the Apple Watch Series 8 will notify you by vibrating on your wrist and displaying the caller's name or number on the screen. This feature is especially helpful when your iPhone is not immediately accessible, such as when it's in another room or in your bag.

To answer the call, simply tap the green phone icon on the screen. The Apple Watch Series 8 will connect the call, allowing you to have a conversation through the watch's speaker and microphone. The call interface will provide options to mute the call, switch to your iPhone, or end the call.

On the other hand, if you wish to decline the call, tap the red phone icon. The watch will send the call to voicemail, and you can review the missed call later on your iPhone.

In situations where you can't take the call at that moment but still want to acknowledge it, you can tap 'Message' to send a predefined text message to the caller, such as "I'll call you later" or "Can't talk right now." Additionally, you can tap 'Remind Me' to set a reminder to call the person back at a specific time or location.

Troubleshooting Call Issues

Sometimes, technical glitches or connectivity issues may interfere with your ability to make or receive calls on your Apple Watch Series 8. If you encounter any difficulties, here are some troubleshooting steps you can follow:

a) **Check Connection**: Ensure that your Apple Watch is connected to your iPhone via Bluetooth. If not, open the Settings app on your Apple Watch, go to Bluetooth, and make sure Bluetooth is turned on. On your iPhone, ensure Bluetooth is also enabled.
b) **Restart Devices**: Restart both your Apple Watch Series 8 and your paired iPhone. Power off, then power on both devices to refresh their systems and potentially resolve any connectivity issues.

c) **Check Call Settings**: Verify that your call settings are configured correctly on your Apple Watch and iPhone. Go to the Watch app on your iPhone, tap 'Phone,' and ensure the settings align with your preferences.
d) **Update Software**: Make sure your Apple Watch Series 8 and iPhone have the latest software updates installed. Outdated software can sometimes cause compatibility issues.
e) **Contact Apple Support**: If the problem persists, reach out to Apple Support for further assistance. They can provide guidance and troubleshoot the issue to ensure your calling feature functions optimally.

Mastering the art of making and receiving calls on the Apple Watch Series 8 is an empowering experience, especially for seniors who value staying connected with their network. This section has provided a comprehensive, step-by-step guide to navigating this essential feature. From initiating a call by accessing contacts or using Siri to answering and managing incoming calls, the Apple Watch Series 8 simplifies communication and ensures seniors can always reach out to their loved ones or seek assistance when needed.

Sending Messages

Sending a Text Message

In our digitally connected world, the ability to send and receive messages swiftly and effortlessly is an essential feature of any smart device, especially for seniors who seek to stay in touch with their loved ones. The Apple Watch Series 8, with its intuitive interface and practical design, makes sending text messages a breeze. This section will provide a detailed guide on how to send a text message using your Apple Watch Series 8.

1. Start by raising your wrist to wake up your Apple Watch Series 8. Alternatively, tap the screen or press the digital crown or side button. The vibrant display will illuminate, presenting you with the watch face or the last app you were using.
2. The Messages app is represented by a green speech bubble icon. You can find this app on your app grid, which you can access by tapping the app icons or using the digital crown to zoom out into the grid view.
3. Tap the Messages app icon to open the application. As you tap, the app will launch, and you will be directed to the main Messages screen.
4. To compose a new message, tap the '+' button, usually located in the top right corner. This action will initiate a new message composition screen, ready for you to begin composing your message.
5. You have the option to select a recipient for your message. Tap the '+' button or the 'Add Contact' icon to access your contacts. From there, you can either scroll through your contact list or use the digital crown to navigate more efficiently. Alternatively, you can use Siri by saying, "Hey Siri, send a message to [contact name]."
6. After selecting a recipient, you can start composing your message. The Apple Watch Series 8 offers various input methods for composing your text, including dictation, scribbling, or using the keyboard.
    - **Dictation**: Tap the microphone icon and speak your message clearly. The Apple Watch will transcribe your words into text.

- **Scribble**: Tap the Scribble button and use your finger to write each letter of your message on the screen. The Apple Watch will convert your scribbles into text.
- **Keyboard**: Tap the keyboard icon, and a keyboard will appear on the screen. Use the digital crown to select letters and type out your message.

7. The Messages app on the Apple Watch Series 8 also allows you to format your text and insert emojis to add expression to your messages. You can access these options within the compose message screen.
    - **Formatting**: Tap the 'Aa' icon to toggle through text formatting options such as bold, italics, underline, and more.
    - **Emojis**: Tap the smiley face icon to access a selection of emojis. Scroll through the options and tap an emoji to add it to your message.
8. Once you have composed your message and are satisfied with it, tap the 'Send' button. The Apple Watch Series 8 will then dispatch your message to the intended recipient.

Replying to a Message

Receiving a message on your Apple Watch Series 8 is simple and efficient. When a new message arrives, a notification will pop up on your watch, displaying the sender's name or phone number and a preview of the message.

1. To view the received message, raise your wrist, tap the screen, or press the digital crown or side button to wake your Apple Watch Series 8.
2. Tap the notification or locate the Messages app icon (green speech bubble) on your app grid, then tap it to open the Messages app.
3. Upon entering the Messages app, you'll see a list of recent conversations. Tap the conversation containing the message you want to view.
4. The message will be displayed on the screen. To reply, tap 'Reply.' You can choose to reply using dictation, predefined responses, scribbling, or the keyboard, similar to the methods described earlier for composing a new message.
5. Once you've composed your reply, tap 'Send.' The Apple Watch Series 8 will then send your response to the original sender.

Incorporating the Message Features

Apart from sending and replying to messages, the Apple Watch Series 8 allows users to utilize additional features within the Messages app, enhancing the overall messaging experience.

Audio Messages

To send an audio message, tap and hold the microphone icon (usually to the right of the text input area) and record your message. Release the icon when you've finished recording, and the message will be sent automatically.

Digital Touch

Digital Touch allows you to send sketches, taps, and even your heartbeat. To use this feature, tap the heart icon and use your finger to create a digital touch message.

Animoji and Memoji

If you're feeling playful, tap the App Store icon within the Messages app, then tap the Animoji or Memoji icon. Select an Animoji or Memoji and record a message using its facial expressions and your voice.

Sending and receiving messages with the Apple Watch Series 8 is a straightforward and user-friendly process, allowing seniors to stay connected with friends and family effortlessly. With its array of input options and additional messaging features, the Apple Watch Series 8 enriches the messaging experience for seniors, ensuring they can maintain meaningful connections in our digital world.

Using Emergency SOS

In a rapidly evolving digital landscape, the Apple Watch Series 8 stands as a beacon of safety and security for its users. One of its most crucial features in this regard is the Emergency SOS function, designed to provide immediate assistance and summon aid in times of distress. For seniors, this feature is particularly vital, offering peace of mind and a sense of security, knowing that help is just a few taps away. In this section, we will delve into the intricacies of using Emergency SOS on the Apple Watch Series 8, exploring its activation, cancellation, customization, and other essential aspects.

Initiating an Emergency SOS

The Emergency SOS feature on the Apple Watch Series 8 is ingeniously designed to be easily accessible and intuitive to use, especially in emergencies. Activating it is a straightforward process:

1. To initiate an emergency call, press the side button (the larger of the two physical buttons on the right side of the watch) rapidly five times in a row. The side button is identifiable by its distinctive shape and position.
2. After the fifth press, the Apple Watch Series 8 will display an emergency countdown screen accompanied by a loud alarm. This countdown provides a few moments for you to cancel the emergency call if it was activated accidentally.
3. If the countdown is not canceled within the stipulated time, the watch will automatically initiate a call to emergency services based on your location. This ensures that help is dispatched to your precise location swiftly.

Simultaneously, the watch will also send a notification to your designated emergency contacts, informing them of the emergency and providing them with your location details.

Canceling an Emergency SOS

While the Emergency SOS feature is vital for ensuring timely assistance during emergencies, there might be instances where you accidentally trigger it or no longer require assistance. Canceling the Emergency SOS is just as crucial as activating it:

1. If you've unintentionally initiated the Emergency SOS or if the situation changes and you no longer need emergency assistance, tap the 'Cancel' option on the screen.

2. Tapping 'Cancel' halts the countdown and prevents the automatic call to emergency services. This action ensures that help is not dispatched when it's no longer necessary.
3. It's vital to use the 'Cancel' function responsibly to avoid any unnecessary distress to emergency services. Accidental activations are not uncommon, and understanding how to cancel the process promptly is essential.

Customizing Emergency SOS Settings

To tailor the Emergency SOS feature to your specific needs and preferences, the Apple Watch Series 8 allows users to customize certain settings related to this functionality:

Adding Emergency Contacts

It's crucial to designate emergency contacts in the Apple Health app on the connected iPhone. These contacts will be notified automatically when Emergency SOS is triggered, providing them with essential information about the situation and your location.

Customizing SOS Contacts

Open the Apple Watch app on your iPhone and navigate to the 'My Watch' tab. Tap 'General' and then 'Emergency SOS.' Here, you can add or remove emergency contacts to ensure the right individuals are notified during an emergency.

Enabling Fall Detection

For added safety, consider enabling fall detection, which can automatically trigger an Emergency SOS call if the watch detects a significant fall and you're immobile for a minute.

Disabling Auto Call

If you prefer not to have your Apple Watch Series 8 automatically dial emergency services after the countdown, you can disable the 'Hold to Auto Call' option in the Emergency SOS settings. This allows you to initiate the call manually after the countdown.

When to Use Emergency SOS

Understanding the appropriate situations to utilize the Emergency SOS feature is paramount in optimizing its functionality and benefits:

Medical Emergencies

Emergency SOS is indispensable in medical emergencies such as cardiac issues, severe allergic reactions, or any situation where immediate medical attention is required.

Accidents and Falls

In case of a fall or accident that leaves you incapacitated, Emergency SOS can be a lifeline, ensuring that help is dispatched promptly.

Threatening Situations

If you find yourself in a dangerous or threatening situation, utilizing Emergency SOS can connect you to emergency services for assistance and protection.

Unexpected Circumstances

Any unforeseen circumstance where immediate help is necessary, whether it's a fire, natural disaster, or any event posing a significant risk, warrants the use of Emergency SOS.

Educating Seniors on Emergency SOS

For seniors, understanding and becoming proficient in using the Emergency SOS feature is critical. Here are steps to educate and ensure their comfort and confidence in utilizing this life-saving tool:

1. Encourage seniors to practice activating and canceling the Emergency SOS feature under your guidance, ensuring they are comfortable with the process.
2. Repeat the steps and reinforce the information, highlighting the importance of this feature and when to use it. Emphasize that accidental activations can be canceled promptly.
3. Engage in role-playing scenarios to simulate emergencies, guiding seniors on when and how to use the Emergency SOS feature effectively.
4. Regularly review and update the designated emergency contacts to ensure the information is current and accurate.

The Emergency SOS feature on the Apple Watch Series 8 is a remarkable tool designed to enhance safety and provide immediate assistance during emergencies. For seniors, mastering the activation, cancellation, and customization of this feature is pivotal, empowering them to confidently utilize their Apple Watch for their well-being. By understanding the steps involved and the appropriate situations to employ Emergency SOS, seniors can embrace the enhanced security and peace of mind that this feature offers, making the Apple Watch Series 8 a valuable companion in their daily lives.

CHAPTER 4

PRACTICAL APPLICATIONS

In this chapter, we delve into the practical applications of the Apple Watch Series 8, a remarkable technological companion designed with seniors in mind. The focus is on enhancing everyday productivity and organization through setting reminders and alarms, effectively using the calendar, and managing notifications. We'll take you through each process step-by-step, ensuring a seamless integration of these features into your daily routine.

Setting Reminders and Alarms

In our bustling world, where time is of the essence, keeping track of important tasks and events is crucial. For seniors, having an efficient and user-friendly way to set reminders and alarms can significantly enhance their daily routines. The Apple Watch Series 8 offers an accessible and convenient solution to this need, allowing seniors to organize their schedules and never miss an appointment. In this section, we will delve into the intricacies of setting reminders and alarms on the Apple Watch Series 8, outlining step-by-step instructions to make the process simple and seamless.

Accessing the Reminders App

To initiate the process of setting reminders on the Apple Watch Series 8, locate and tap the "Reminders" app on the home screen. The app icon typically features a checklist or reminder icon, making it easily recognizable among other applications. A single tap on this icon will launch the app, preparing you to create reminders effortlessly.

Upon entering the Reminders app, the interface is typically divided into various sections, displaying any existing reminders and providing options to add new ones. The clean and intuitive design of the app ensures that seniors can navigate and interact with it without any confusion, setting a solid foundation for managing their tasks effectively.

Creating a Reminder

To create a reminder, tap the "+" button typically positioned in the app's interface. This action prompts the app to open a blank template where you can input the details of the reminder. Begin by typing in the task or event you want to be reminded of. For instance, you might input "Doctor's appointment" or "Take medication."

Once you've specified the task, proceed to set a due date and time for the reminder. The Apple Watch Series 8 allows for precise time settings, ensuring you can align the reminder with your schedule accurately. For a reminder regarding a doctor's appointment, setting the due date and time to match the appointment details is pivotal.

Setting Alarms

In addition to reminders, setting alarms is a vital aspect of managing time efficiently. Alarms serve as an audible alert that ensures you don't overlook crucial events or deadlines. To set an alarm on the Apple Watch Series 8, locate and tap the "Clock" app on the home screen.

Within the Clock app, search for the "+" button, typically situated in a noticeable location to facilitate easy access. Tapping this button triggers the creation of a new alarm. Once inside the alarm creation interface, set the time by scrolling through the available options, usually displayed in an intuitive digital or analog clock format.

Additionally, the Apple Watch Series 8 offers the option to repeat alarms, ensuring you can set them for specific days of the week or customize the recurrence pattern based on your preferences. This flexibility is particularly beneficial for seniors who may have regular medical check-ups or events that follow a consistent schedule.

Utilizing Voice Commands

Seniors may find using voice commands exceptionally convenient and efficient. The Apple Watch Series 8 integrates Siri, Apple's voice-activated assistant, which can handle reminders and alarms based on vocal instructions. Activating Siri is as simple as pressing and holding the digital crown, prompting Siri to listen for your command.

To set a reminder using voice commands, state, "Hey Siri, set a reminder for [task] at [time]." Siri will process your instruction and create the reminder accordingly, eliminating the need for manual input and streamlining the process, especially for seniors who may prefer voice interaction over typing.

The ability to set reminders and alarms swiftly and accurately is a remarkable feature of the Apple Watch Series 8, making it an indispensable tool for seniors. Whether through the traditional method of manual input or the modern convenience of voice commands, the watch ensures that important events and tasks are never overlooked, enhancing productivity and aiding in efficient time management. As we move forward, we'll explore yet another essential aspect of organization and time management: using the calendar application.

Using the Calendar

The Calendar application on the Apple Watch Series 8 is a powerful tool that can significantly improve how seniors manage their time and stay organized. Its seamless integration with the iPhone and its user-friendly interface makes it an indispensable feature for keeping track of events, appointments, and commitments. In this section, we will explore in-depth how to utilize the Calendar application to its fullest potential.

Accessing the Calendar App

Accessing the Calendar application is straightforward. Simply raise your wrist to activate the Apple Watch or tap on the watch face to wake it up. Once awake, locate and tap the "Calendar" app icon, usually represented by a stylized calendar icon among the other app icons on the home screen. Tapping this icon will launch the Calendar application, giving you an instant overview of your scheduled events and appointments.

Viewing and Adding Events

Viewing Events

Upon launching the Calendar application, you will be presented with a clear and easy-to-read view of the current month. Events and appointments are typically denoted by colored dots or markings on the respective dates. Tap on a specific date to view the events scheduled for that day.

To navigate through different dates and months, swipe left or right on the screen. This gesture allows you to quickly move between months, enabling you to plan ahead or review past events effortlessly.

When you tap on a date with scheduled events, a list or visual representation of the events for that day will appear. Tapping on a particular event provides more details, such as the event's title, time, location, and any notes you may have added.

Adding a New Event:

1. To add a new event, tap the "+" button, usually located at the top or bottom of the screen. This action will open a new event window where you can input event details.
2. Fill in the event title, location (if applicable), start and end times, and any notes that are relevant to the event. For recurring events, toggle the "Repeat" option and choose the appropriate repetition pattern (daily, weekly, monthly, etc.).
3. You can set alerts to remind you of the event beforehand. These alerts can be customized to your preference, ensuring you are reminded at a suitable time.
4. Once you have provided all the necessary details, tap "Add" or "Save" to confirm and add the event to your calendar.

Syncing with iPhone

One of the most convenient features of the Apple Watch Series 8 is its seamless integration with your iPhone's calendar. Any event or appointment you add, edit, or delete on your iPhone is automatically synchronized with your Apple Watch, and vice versa. This synchronization ensures that you always have the most up-to-date schedule on your wrist.

To maximize the benefits of this synchronization:

Ensure iCloud Sync is Enabled

On your iPhone, go to Settings > [Your Name] > iCloud, and make sure the "Calendars" option is toggled on. This allows events created on your iPhone to be seamlessly synced with your Apple Watch.

Check Calendar Settings on Apple Watch

On your Apple Watch, go to Settings > Calendar and confirm that "Mirror my iPhone" is enabled. This setting ensures that changes made on your iPhone are reflected on your watch.

Using Siri for Event Creation

Utilize Siri by holding the digital crown and saying, "Hey Siri, add an event to my calendar for [date and time] called [event name]." Siri will promptly create the event for you, further streamlining the process.

Other Useful Features

Searching for Events

In the Calendar application, you can easily search for specific events by tapping the magnifying glass icon and entering relevant keywords or phrases. This feature is particularly useful when you have a busy schedule and need to find a specific event quickly.

Editing and Deleting Events

To edit or delete an event, navigate to the event details and tap "Edit." From here, you can make the necessary changes or tap "Delete Event" to remove it from your calendar.

Switching Between Views

The Calendar app allows you to switch between different views, including day, week, month, and year views. Simply tap on the corresponding view icon (day, week, month) to switch to the desired view and get a different perspective of your schedule.

Mastering the use of the Calendar application on the Apple Watch Series 8 provides seniors with a powerful tool to manage their time efficiently and keep track of their engagements. With its intuitive interface and seamless integration with the iPhone, staying organized has never been more accessible. By following these detailed steps and utilizing the provided tips, seniors can fully utilize the potential of the Calendar application, making their lives more organized and productive.

Managing Notifications

Efficiently managing notifications on your Apple Watch Series 8 is essential for maintaining focus and staying organized in this digital age. The watch is designed to provide timely alerts for various apps and activities, but personalizing these notifications according to your preferences can significantly enhance your user experience. In this section, we'll delve into the depths of managing notifications step by step, ensuring you have complete control over what alerts you receive and how you receive them.

Accessing Notification Settings

To embark on the journey of finely tuning your notifications, begin by accessing the "Settings" app on your Apple Watch Series 8. This is your gateway to customizing and controlling the notifications that reach your wrist.

1. On the watch's home screen, look for the icon that resembles a gear representing the Settings app.
2. Tap on the Settings icon to enter the world of personalized settings and preferences.
3. Scroll through the available options within the Settings app and locate the "Notifications" section. This is where the magic of managing notifications happens.

Customizing Notifications

Within the Notifications section, you'll find a list of apps installed on your Apple Watch Series 8. Each app can be individually configured to provide notifications in a manner that suits your lifestyle and needs.

1. Scroll through the list of apps and choose the one you wish to customize. For example, you might want to start with Messages, Email, or any other frequently used app.
2. Once you select an app, you'll have the option to customize various notification preferences, including sound, haptics, and notification display options.
    - **Sound**: Choose the notification sound that suits your preference. Whether you like a subtle ping or a more attention-grabbing tone, the choice is yours.
    - **Haptics**: Haptics refers to the vibrations your watch produces with each notification. Adjust the intensity of these vibrations to match your comfort level.

- **Notification Display**: Decide how you want the notifications to be displayed—whether you prefer a simple notification on the watch face or a more detailed view.

3. Repeat the customization process for other apps listed in the Notifications section. Tailor the settings for every app according to its importance and relevance to your daily routine.

By customizing notifications for each app, you ensure that you're only alerted to what truly matters to you. Unnecessary or disruptive notifications can be minimized, providing a smoother and less distracting experience with your Apple Watch.

Enabling Do Not Disturb

There are times when you need uninterrupted focus, such as during meetings, important tasks, or when you're winding down for the day. The "Do Not Disturb" feature on the Apple Watch Series 8 is a valuable tool for these moments.

1. Swipe up on the watch face to access the Control Center, where you'll find various essential settings.
2. Look for the crescent moon icon, which symbolizes "Do Not Disturb." Tap the icon to enable this mode.
3. You can further customize the "Do Not Disturb" settings by pressing firmly on the watch face while in the Control Center. Adjust the duration or set it until you leave your current location, ensuring you're undisturbed as needed.

"Do Not Disturb" ensures a peaceful and distraction-free environment when necessary, allowing you to focus on the task at hand or enjoy moments of tranquility.

Utilizing Theater Mode

Theater Mode is another handy feature designed to minimize distractions, especially in dark or quiet environments like a theater or a meeting.

1. Swipe up on the watch face to access the Control Center.
2. Look for the mask icon, which symbolizes Theater Mode. Tap the icon to enable this mode.
3. When Theater Mode is activated, your Apple Watch Series 8 will remain silent and will not light up the screen when you receive notifications. However, you can still feel haptic alerts.

Theater Mode ensures you don't disturb others with bright screen notifications and loud sounds, enhancing your consideration for those around you.

Managing Notification Groups (if available)

Depending on your watch's software version and features, you may have the option to manage notifications using groups, a further level of organization.

1. **Access the Notification Groups Settings**: If available, navigate within the Notifications section to find the option to manage notification groups.
2. **Create or Edit Groups**: You can create new groups or edit existing ones to group specific types of notifications together. This way, you can have separate groups for work-related apps, personal apps, or any other categorization that suits your needs.

3. **Customize Group Settings**: Adjust the notification preferences for each group, similar to customizing individual app notifications. Tailor sound, haptics, and notification display to match the group's relevance.

Notification groups allow for a more organized and streamlined notification experience, enabling you to quickly identify and respond to notifications based on their importance and category.

Managing notifications on your Apple Watch Series 8 is a pivotal aspect of maximizing its potential as a productive and unobtrusive companion. By customizing notifications, enabling "Do Not Disturb," utilizing Theater Mode, and possibly managing notification groups, you can strike a balance between staying informed and maintaining focused tranquility. Mastering these notification management techniques ensures that your Apple Watch Series 8 seamlessly integrates into your daily routine, enhancing both productivity and peace of mind.

CHAPTER 5

ADVANCED FEATURES

The Apple Watch Series 8 offers a myriad of advanced features, making it a valuable companion for seniors seeking to monitor their health and enhance their overall well-being. In this comprehensive guide, we will delve into Chapter 5, focusing on three key features: ECG and Blood Oxygen Monitoring, Fall Detection, and utilizing Third-Party Apps. By the end of this guide, you will have a thorough understanding of how to effectively use these features and tailor them to your specific needs and preferences.

ECG and Blood Oxygen Monitoring

ECG (Electrocardiogram) Monitoring

One of the standout features of the Apple Watch Series 8 is its ability to perform an Electrocardiogram (ECG), a test that measures the electrical activity of your heart. This feature is of immense importance for seniors as it can help in detecting irregular heart rhythms, such as atrial fibrillation, allowing for early intervention and necessary medical attention. To utilize this feature optimally, follow these detailed steps:

1. **Ensure Proper Fit**: Begin by wearing your Apple Watch snugly on your wrist, ensuring it is in the correct position and maintaining good skin contact. A secure fit is essential for accurate readings.
2. **Open the ECG App**: Locate and tap on the ECG app on your Apple Watch. The app is typically denoted by an icon resembling a waveform. Upon tapping, the app will initiate, ready to record your heart's electrical activity.
3. **Rest Your Arm**: Place your arm, the one wearing the Apple Watch, on a stable surface such as a table or your lap. This helps to minimize any unnecessary movement during the reading.
4. **Follow On-screen Instructions**: The app will provide clear and easy-to-follow on-screen instructions to guide you through the ECG recording process. Typically, this involves holding your finger on the Digital Crown of the Apple Watch.
5. **Record the ECG**: Follow the prompts to record the ECG. The Watch will analyze your heart's electrical activity over a specific duration, usually 30 seconds, and generate a comprehensive report.
6. **Review the Results**: After the recording is complete, the results can be viewed on your paired iPhone using the Health app. This data is crucial and can be shared with your healthcare professional for further assessment and consultation.

Blood Oxygen Monitoring

Another valuable health monitoring feature on the Apple Watch Series 8 is Blood Oxygen Monitoring. This function is instrumental in assessing blood oxygen levels, which is crucial for overall health. Proper blood oxygen levels ensure that all body tissues and organs receive adequate oxygen for optimal functioning. Here's how to effectively utilize this feature:

1. **Wear the Watch Appropriately**: Like with the ECG feature, ensure that the Apple Watch is snug on your wrist and well-positioned for accurate readings. A comfortable and secure fit is essential.
2. **Locate the Blood Oxygen App**: Find and tap on the Blood Oxygen app on your Apple Watch. The app icon usually depicts a blood droplet. Once located, tap to open the app.
3. **Remain Still and Calm**: To obtain precise readings, remain still and keep your wrist steady during the reading. Any unnecessary movement can affect the accuracy of the measurement.
4. **Initiate the Measurement**: Follow the app's instructions to start the blood oxygen measurement. The Watch's advanced sensors will analyze your blood oxygen saturation level, providing you with an accurate reading.
5. **View the Results**: Once the measurement is complete, the results will be displayed on the screen. Normal blood oxygen levels typically range from 95-100%. If your reading falls within this range, it indicates healthy blood oxygen saturation.
6. **Monitor Trends**: Utilize the Health app on your paired iPhone to track and analyze trends in your blood oxygen levels over time. Monitoring trends can provide valuable insights into your overall health and well-being.

By following these step-by-step instructions, seniors can effectively utilize the ECG and Blood Oxygen Monitoring features on the Apple Watch Series 8, empowering them to monitor their heart health and blood oxygen levels conveniently and accurately.

Fall Detection

Fall Detection is a pivotal safety feature integrated into the Apple Watch Series 8, designed to automatically detect falls and initiate emergency assistance if needed. This feature is particularly crucial for seniors, as accidental falls can have severe consequences. Fall Detection provides peace of mind and ensures prompt medical attention in case of a fall. To set up and use Fall Detection proficiently, follow these comprehensive steps:

1. **Access the Settings**: Begin by opening the Watch app on your paired iPhone and navigating to the 'My Watch' tab.
2. **Select Emergency SOS**: Locate and tap on 'Emergency SOS' from the list of options available in the 'My Watch' tab.
3. **Enable Fall Detection**: To activate Fall Detection, toggle the Fall Detection switch to the 'on' position. Additionally, you may choose to enable 'Hold to Call' for added convenience.
4. **Configure Emergency Contacts**: Set up your emergency contacts within the Emergency SOS settings. Ensure that the appropriate individuals, such as family members or close friends, are added as emergency contacts.
5. **Test Fall Detection**: After configuring the settings, safely simulate a fall to verify that Fall Detection is working correctly. The Apple Watch will prompt you to confirm if you're okay or if you need assistance.
6. **Seek Assistance**: If you are unable to respond or confirm that you're okay, the Apple Watch will automatically call emergency services and notify your designated emergency contacts, providing them with your location for immediate assistance.

By meticulously following these steps, seniors can set up Fall Detection on their Apple Watch Series 8, enhancing their safety and ensuring timely assistance in case of falls or emergencies.

Using Third-Party Apps

The Apple Watch Series 8 is not only a powerful health monitoring device but also a versatile platform that supports a vast array of third-party apps. These apps extend the functionality of the Apple Watch, catering to various needs and interests, and can be particularly beneficial for seniors. From health and fitness apps to communication and entertainment, there's an app for almost every requirement. Here's a detailed guide on how to download, install, and effectively use third-party apps on your Apple Watch Series 8:

1. **Access the App Store**: Begin by opening the App Store app on your paired iPhone. The App Store is the central hub for all available applications compatible with your Apple Watch.
2. **Search for Apps**: Use the search bar at the bottom of the App Store to look for apps that align with your preferences and requirements. You can search for specific categories such as health, fitness, medication reminders, weather updates, and more.
3. **Download the App**: Once you find an app that fits your needs, tap on the app's icon to view its details. Here, you'll find information about the app, including user ratings and reviews. To download and install the app, tap the download icon (usually a cloud icon with an arrow) if it's a free app or the price icon if it's a paid app.

4. **Check Apple Watch Compatibility**: Before downloading, ensure that the app is compatible with the Apple Watch. This information is available on the app's details page in the App Store.
5. **Install the App**: The app will begin to download and install on your iPhone. The process may take a few seconds to a few minutes, depending on the app's size and your internet connection.
6. **Open the App on Your Watch**: After the app is successfully installed on your iPhone, it will automatically sync to your Apple Watch, provided you have enabled this option in your Apple Watch settings. To access the app on your Apple Watch, simply navigate to the app grid or use Siri to open the app.
7. **Use the App**: Tap on the app icon to open and use it directly from your Apple Watch. Most apps have been optimized for a seamless experience on the Watch, providing essential features and functionalities on a smaller, wearable screen.

By following these detailed steps, seniors can explore and utilize a diverse range of third-party apps tailored to their preferences and requirements, thereby maximizing the utility and potential of their Apple Watch Series 8.

The Apple Watch Series 8 boasts an array of advanced features that are incredibly beneficial for seniors. ECG and Blood Oxygen Monitoring offer critical health insights, Fall Detection enhances safety, and integrating third-party apps extends the Watch's capabilities and usefulness. By comprehending and effectively utilizing these features, seniors can significantly improve their health monitoring and overall quality of life, thereby embracing the technological advancements that the Apple Watch Series 8 brings to their fingertips.

CHAPTER 6

SENIORS' FITNESS AND WELLNESS

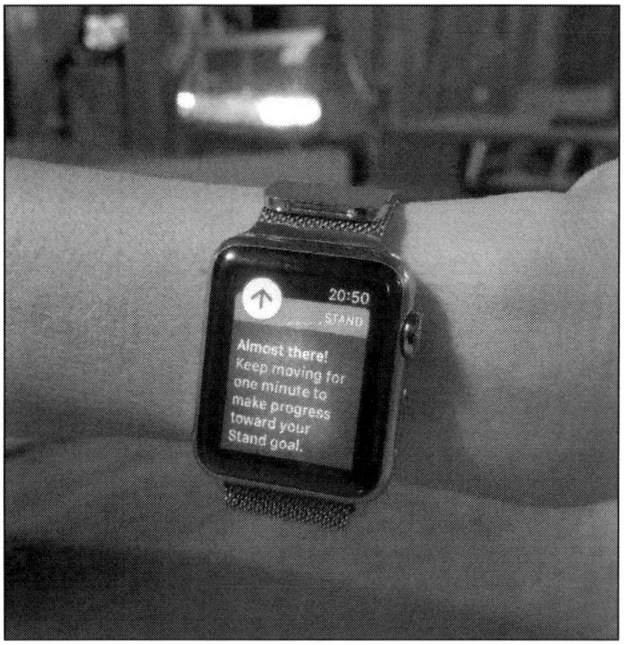

The Apple Watch Series 8 is a remarkable piece of technology that has revolutionized the way seniors manage their fitness and overall wellness. In Chapter 6 of the "Apple Watch Series 8 Seniors Guide," we delve into essential aspects of seniors' fitness and wellness. This chapter covers creating and tracking fitness goals, utilizing sleep-tracking features, and effectively managing medications to ensure a healthier and more active lifestyle for seniors.

Creating and Tracking Fitness Goals

In the pursuit of a healthier and more active lifestyle, setting clear and attainable fitness goals is paramount. These objectives should be rooted in individual capabilities and tailored to factors such as age, health condition, and daily routines. Fitness goals can vary greatly, from achieving a specific number of daily steps to working on more intricate targets like enhancing cardiovascular health or strength training.

Setting Up Fitness Goals on Apple Watch

1. Open the Fitness app on your Apple Watch or the iPhone paired with it.
2. Navigate to the "Activity" tab and select "Set Your Move Goal."
3. Choose a calorie goal that aligns with your fitness aspirations and takes into account your physical capabilities.
4. The Apple Watch Series 8 will continuously monitor your progress, offering real-time updates on your goal achievement throughout the day.

Utilizing the Workout App for Specific Goals

The Apple Watch Series 8's Workout app is a versatile tool that caters to a wide range of fitness goals. It provides various exercise options, from walking and running to cycling, yoga, and more. To make the most of it:

1. Explore the "Workout" app on your Apple Watch, which offers an array of exercise types.
2. Select the specific workout type that aligns with your fitness goals.
3. Set goals for each workout session, such as duration, distance, or calorie expenditure, to closely track your progress and gradually improve your fitness.

Monitoring Progress and Adjusting Goals

Regularly assessing your fitness data within the Fitness app is essential to gauge your progress towards your fitness goals. It helps to maintain motivation and ensure that your objectives remain challenging yet attainable.

1. Review your fitness data to evaluate your progress.
2. Consider modifying your fitness goals if you find them too easy or overly demanding. Adapting goals to your evolving capabilities keeps you engaged and motivated.

Sleep Tracking

Adequate and restorative sleep is vital for seniors' overall health and well-being. Sleep plays a significant role in memory consolidation, immune function, and emotional stability. The Apple Watch Series 8 offers advanced sleep-tracking features to help you optimize your sleep patterns.

Activating Sleep Tracking on Apple Watch

1. Open the "Health" app on your paired iPhone.
2. Go to the "Browse" tab and select "Sleep."
3. Tap "Get Started" to configure your sleep schedule and goals.

Analyzing Sleep Data

After each night's sleep, the Apple Watch Series 8 collects a wealth of data, including time spent in bed, time asleep, heart rate fluctuations, and more. This information serves as a valuable resource to improve the quality and duration of your sleep.

1. Review the sleep data recorded by your Apple Watch Series 8.
2. Pay close attention to patterns in your sleep, including the duration of deep and light sleep phases.
3. Utilize this data to make adjustments to your sleep schedule, bedtime routine, and other factors that may affect your sleep quality.

Improving Sleep Hygiene

Beyond tracking sleep, the Apple Watch Series 8 also encourages good sleep hygiene practices. Here are some tips:

1. Establish a consistent sleep schedule by going to bed and waking up at the same time each day.
2. Create a relaxing bedtime routine to signal to your body that it's time to sleep. This may include reading, light stretching, or calming music.
3. Keep your bedroom dark, quiet, and at a comfortable temperature to promote restful sleep.

Managing Medications

Effective medication management is crucial for seniors to maintain their health. The Apple Watch Series 8 can help streamline this process by organizing medication information and sending timely reminders to ensure medication adherence.

Utilizing the Health App for Medication Tracking

1. Open the "Health" app on your paired iPhone.
2. Navigate to the "Browse" tab and select "Medications."
3. Add your medications, including dosage, frequency, and any special instructions provided by your healthcare provider.

Setting Medication Reminders

1. Configure reminders for each medication you take, specifying the time and frequency for alerts.
2. The Apple Watch Series 8 will provide gentle reminders at the designated times to take your medications, promoting consistency and adherence to your prescribed regimen.

Reviewing Medication Compliance

Regularly reviewing your medication compliance through the Health app is crucial for ensuring that you're taking your medications as prescribed by your healthcare provider. This feature also enables you to share accurate medication information during consultations.

1. Use the Health app to verify that you've taken your medications according to your prescribed schedule.
2. If you have any concerns or uncertainties about your medications, consult with your healthcare provider promptly.

Medication Safety Tips

In addition to managing medications with the help of your Apple Watch Series 8, it's essential to follow these safety guidelines:

1. Keep all medications in their original containers with clear labels.
2. Store medications in a cool, dry place, away from direct sunlight and extreme temperatures.
3. Keep medications out of reach of children and pets.
4. Dispose of expired or unused medications properly, following local guidelines or pharmaceutical take-back programs.

While the Apple Watch Series 8 is a valuable tool for medication management, it should complement, not replace, the guidance of healthcare professionals. Always consult with your doctor or pharmacist if you have any questions or concerns about your medications.

Harnessing the power of the Apple Watch Series 8 for seniors' fitness and wellness involves setting and tracking personalized fitness goals, optimizing sleep patterns through advanced sleep-tracking features, and efficiently managing medications. By following the step-by-step guidance provided in this chapter, seniors can enhance their overall well-being and lead a healthier, more active lifestyle, empowered by the advanced capabilities of the Apple Watch Series 8. Whether it's achieving fitness milestones, improving sleep quality, or ensuring medication adherence, the Apple Watch Series 8 serves as a valuable companion on the journey to better health and wellness for seniors.

CHAPTER 7

TROUBLESHOOTING AND TIPS

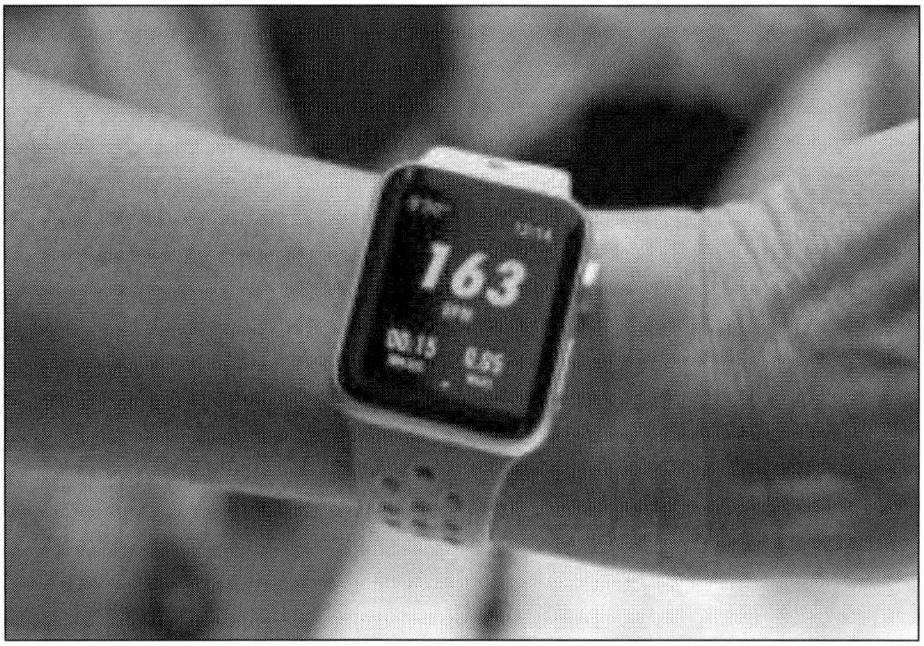

In the ever-evolving world of technology, the Apple Watch Series 8 stands as a marvel of innovation, delivering an array of features that enhance the lives of seniors. However, as with any sophisticated device, occasional hiccups and challenges may arise. This chapter, titled "Troubleshooting and Tips," aims to provide a comprehensive guide to address common issues that seniors might encounter while using their Apple Watch Series 8. Additionally, we'll explore strategies to maximize battery life, an essential aspect of ensuring uninterrupted usage. Lastly, we'll delve into resources that can offer further assistance and guidance, allowing seniors to make the most of their wearable technology.

Common Issues and Solutions

The Apple Watch Series 8 is a powerful device, but like any piece of technology, it can encounter issues. It's crucial to understand these common problems and how to troubleshoot them effectively, ensuring a smooth and uninterrupted user experience.

Connectivity Issues

Connectivity problems can disrupt the seamless functionality of the Apple Watch. If you're facing issues with connecting to your iPhone or Wi-Fi, start by ensuring that both devices have Bluetooth and Wi-Fi turned on. If the problem persists, try restarting both devices, as a simple reboot can often resolve connectivity hiccups.

Sometimes, forgetfulness or accidentally turning off these features can lead to connectivity problems. Verifying that Bluetooth and Wi-Fi are indeed active on both the watch and the paired iPhone is a fundamental step. For Bluetooth, it's also advisable to check for any other nearby devices causing interference.

If basic checks don't resolve the issue, a more advanced step would involve unpairing and re-pairing your Apple Watch with your iPhone. This essentially resets the connection and often helps in establishing a stable and functional link between the devices.

Unresponsive Touch Screen

If your Apple Watch's touch screen is unresponsive, start by giving it a thorough clean to remove any dirt or debris. If cleaning doesn't solve the issue, a restart or a force restart might help. Hold down both the side button and the Digital Crown simultaneously until the Apple logo appears on the screen.

An unresponsive touch screen can be a result of software glitches or hardware issues. Cleaning the screen is a basic yet essential step. If the issue persists, a force restart usually addresses software-related problems. However, if the unresponsiveness persists after a restart, it's advisable to contact Apple Support or visit an Apple Store for further diagnosis.

Additionally, software updates released by Apple can often contain patches or fixes for touchscreen issues. Checking for and installing the latest updates may resolve persistent touchscreen problems.

Battery Drain

Battery drain is a common concern for smartwatch users. To mitigate this, disable unnecessary features such as background app refresh, raise to wake, and excessive notifications. Adjust screen brightness and use a dark watch face to save power. Additionally, monitor and manage battery-intensive apps to optimize battery life.

Battery management is vital for uninterrupted usage throughout the day. Adjusting settings to minimize power consumption, like reducing the screen brightness or utilizing the low power mode, can significantly enhance the battery life. It's also crucial to periodically review and optimize app permissions to ensure that apps aren't using the watch's features excessively, draining the battery.

For seniors, who may rely heavily on specific features, it's beneficial to educate them about the impact of various settings on battery life. This empowers them to make informed decisions based on their usage needs.

App Issues

If you're experiencing problems with a specific app on your Apple Watch, start by checking for updates. Outdated apps can often cause glitches and performance issues. If that doesn't help, try uninstalling and reinstalling the app to ensure a fresh installation.

App-related issues are quite common and can stem from compatibility problems or corrupted installations. Keeping the apps updated ensures that you have the latest bug fixes and improvements. In the case of persistent issues, reach out to the app developer for support or consult Apple's support channels for further assistance.

Seniors might find it helpful to have a step-by-step guide on updating and managing apps, ensuring they can seamlessly enjoy the features of their favorite applications.

Syncing Problems

Sometimes, the Apple Watch may face syncing issues with your iPhone. To troubleshoot this, ensure that both devices are connected to the same Wi-Fi network and have Bluetooth enabled. Restarting both devices and checking for updates can often resolve syncing problems.

Syncing problems can be frustrating, especially when it interferes with essential functionalities. Highlighting the importance of a stable Wi-Fi and Bluetooth connection and guiding users on how to reset network settings or pair the devices again can be immensely beneficial for seniors encountering syncing issues.

Heart Rate Inaccuracies

If you find that your Apple Watch is not accurately measuring your heart rate, make sure the device is snug on your wrist and the sensors are clean. If the issue persists, consider resetting the device and reconfiguring the health settings.

Heart rate monitoring is a critical feature for seniors, especially those monitoring their health closely. Educating them about the correct positioning of the watch and the significance of clean sensors can help in improving the accuracy of heart rate readings. Additionally, emphasizing the importance of a snug fit can lead to better results during workouts or daily activity tracking.

Notification Delays

Delayed notifications can be frustrating. Ensure that your Apple Watch is within the Bluetooth range of your iPhone and that both devices are properly connected. Restarting your devices and checking notification settings can often rectify this issue.

Notifications are crucial for staying updated and connected. Helping seniors understand how to manage notification settings and ensuring a reliable Bluetooth connection can alleviate the frustration caused by delayed or missed notifications.

Maximizing Battery Life

A critical aspect of a positive user experience with the Apple Watch Series 8 is battery life optimization. Implementing specific strategies can significantly extend the time between charges, ensuring that the device is always ready for use when needed.

Optimize Display Settings

Adjusting the display settings can notably impact battery life. Lower the screen brightness and set a shorter screen timeout to conserve power. Utilizing a simple watch face and disabling the "Always On" feature can also help extend battery life.

The display is one of the primary contributors to battery drain. Seniors may benefit from understanding how different display settings affect the battery and how they can tailor these settings to suit their preferences while optimizing battery life.

Manage Notifications

Notifications can drain the battery, especially if you receive them frequently. Review and disable notifications for unnecessary apps, focusing only on the ones that are essential. This minimizes the number of times the screen lights up, thus saving battery power.

Many seniors appreciate assistance in organizing their notifications efficiently. Educating them on how to customize notification settings according to their priorities can lead to more efficient use of the watch and increased battery life.

Limit Background App Refresh

Background app refresh allows apps to update data in the background, consuming battery power. Disable this feature for non-essential apps to preserve battery life. Only enable it for critical apps you need to stay updated.

Seniors may not be aware of how background app refresh affects battery life. A simple explanation of this feature and how to manage it according to their preferences can significantly extend the battery life of their Apple Watch.

Manage App Usage

Keep an eye on apps that consume a significant amount of battery. Use the iPhone companion app to check battery usage, and if needed, limit the usage of power-hungry apps to conserve energy.

Understanding the impact of specific apps on battery life is essential for optimizing usage. Seniors might appreciate guidance on how to monitor app usage and make informed decisions about which apps to limit or use sparingly to preserve battery life.

Enable Power Reserve Mode

When your battery is critically low, activating Power Reserve mode can be a lifesaver. This mode displays only the time and disables all other functions, ensuring your watch remains functional for an extended period until you can charge it.

Power Reserve mode can be a valuable feature for seniors, especially when they are away from a charging source. Providing a step-by-step guide on how to activate and use Power Reserve mode ensures that seniors can continue using their watch for essential functions even during low battery situations.

Utilize Airplane Mode

If you're in a low-service area or don't need constant connectivity, consider enabling Airplane Mode. This turns off cellular and Wi-Fi functions, conserving battery for other essential features.

Seniors may not always require constant connectivity, especially when they're focused on specific activities. Explaining how Airplane Mode works and how to activate it can help seniors manage their watch's connectivity and extend battery life during specific situations.

Resources for Further Assistance

In the age of technology, having access to comprehensive resources and assistance is paramount. Apple has established a robust support system to aid users in resolving issues and understanding the full potential of their devices.

Apple Support Website

Apple's official support website (https://support.apple.com) is a treasure trove of information. Here, you can find step-by-step guides, troubleshooting articles, and videos covering a wide array of topics related to the Apple Watch Series 8.

Encouraging seniors to explore and familiarize themselves with Apple's support website can empower them to troubleshoot issues independently. It's a valuable resource that provides answers to a myriad of questions they might have about their Apple Watch.

Apple Store

Visiting an Apple Store can provide personalized assistance. Apple's dedicated staff can help diagnose and address any issues you may be facing with your Apple Watch Series 8. They can also guide you on how to optimize your device for the best experience.

For seniors who prefer hands-on assistance, a trip to the Apple Store can be highly beneficial. The Apple Store staff can offer tailored advice and demonstrate solutions, creating a positive and educational experience for seniors.

Online Communities

Joining online communities and forums, such as the Apple Support Communities (https://discussions.apple.com), allows you to connect with other Apple Watch users. You can seek advice, share experiences, and learn from a community of like-minded individuals.

Online communities offer a sense of community and shared experiences. For seniors, participating in these forums can provide insights, tips, and solutions from peers, enhancing their understanding and usage of the Apple Watch Series 8.

Third-Party Guides and Books

Utilize books and guides specifically tailored for seniors using the Apple Watch Series 8. These resources often provide easy-to-follow instructions, tips, and troubleshooting techniques, assisting seniors in making the most of their smartwatches.

Third-party guides and books tailored for seniors offer a user-friendly approach to understanding the Apple Watch Series 8. They break down complex concepts into simple, easy-to-follow instructions, making the learning process enjoyable and accessible for seniors.

Understanding and troubleshooting common issues, optimizing battery life, and accessing reliable resources are pivotal elements in ensuring a seamless and fulfilling experience with the Apple Watch Series 8. By addressing challenges effectively and maximizing the potential of this remarkable device, seniors can embrace the benefits of modern technology with confidence and ease. The Apple Watch Series 8 truly stands as a tool that enriches the lives of seniors, offering convenience, health monitoring, and a sense of empowerment in the digital age.

CHAPTER 8

SECURITY AND PRIVACY

In the digital age, personal security and privacy are paramount concerns. With the introduction of the Apple Watch Series 8, Apple has continued to focus on enhancing these aspects. This chapter, "Security and Privacy," in the Apple Watch Series 8 Seniors Guide, will delve deep into the various features and practices you can employ to safeguard your personal data and enable privacy features on your device.

Protecting Personal Data

Passcode Protection

One of the fundamental steps in protecting your Apple Watch's data is setting up a passcode. A passcode acts as the first line of defense against unauthorized access. To set up a passcode on your Apple Watch Series 8, follow these steps:

- Open the "Settings" app on your watch.
- Scroll down and select "Passcode."
- Tap "Turn Passcode On."
- Enter a secure passcode of your choice (a combination of numbers and/or letters).
- Re-enter the passcode to confirm it.

Wrist Detection

Wrist Detection is an intelligent feature that ensures your watch remains unlocked as long as you're wearing it. To enable Wrist Detection:

- Open the "Settings" app on your watch.
- Scroll down and select "Passcode."
- Toggle on the "Wrist Detection" option.

Data Encryption

Apple Watch Series 8 encrypts your data to protect it from prying eyes. The encryption ensures that even if someone gains access to your watch, they won't be able to read the stored data without your passcode or authentication. It's vital to keep your watch updated to maintain the latest security protocols.

App Permissions

Take control of which apps can access your watch's data by managing app permissions:

- Open the "Settings" app on your watch.
- Scroll down and select the app you want to adjust permissions for.
- Review and customize the permissions as needed.

Two-Factor Authentication

To add an extra layer of security to your Apple ID and your Apple Watch, consider enabling Two-Factor Authentication (2FA). This feature requires you to enter a verification code sent to your trusted devices whenever you log in from a new device. To enable 2FA:

- Open the "Settings" app on your paired iPhone.
- Scroll down and select "Password & Security."
- Tap "Two-Factor Authentication" and follow the on-screen instructions.

Find My

The "Find My" feature helps you locate your watch if it's lost or stolen. It also allows you to remotely lock or erase your device to protect your data. To set up and use Find My:

- Open the "Find My" app on your paired iPhone.
- Tap "Devices" and select your Apple Watch Series 8.
- Follow the options for tracking, locking, or erasing your device as needed.

Enabling Privacy Features

Location Services

Your Apple Watch Series 8 utilizes Location Services for various features like Maps and Weather. To ensure your location is not being used without your consent:

- Open the "Settings" app on your watch.
- Scroll down and select "Privacy."
- Tap on "Location Services" and adjust the settings for individual apps or disable it entirely if you prefer.

App Privacy Report

The App Privacy Report is a valuable tool to understand how apps are using your data. It provides insights into which apps have accessed your location, camera, or microphone recently. To check your App Privacy Report:

- On your paired iPhone, go to "Settings."
- Scroll down and select "Privacy."
- Tap on "App Privacy Report" to view the details.

Bluetooth and Wi-Fi Privacy

Apple Watch Series 8 uses Bluetooth and Wi-Fi for various functions. To enhance privacy and security:

- Disable Bluetooth and Wi-Fi when not in use.
- Avoid connecting to unsecured public Wi-Fi networks.

Siri Privacy

Siri is your virtual assistant on the Apple Watch Series 8. To protect your privacy while using Siri:

- Open the "Settings" app on your watch.
- Scroll down and select "Siri."
- Review and adjust the settings for Siri's data usage.

Mail and Messages Privacy

Emails and messages often contain sensitive information. To safeguard your communications:

- Enable "Lock with Passcode" for your Mail and Messages apps.
- Use the built-in privacy features like Hide Alerts and Message Effects for Messages.

Privacy While Exercising

Apple Watch Series 8 offers advanced health and fitness features. To maintain your privacy while tracking your workouts:

- Review the privacy settings for health and fitness data in the "Health" app on your paired iPhone.
- Adjust sharing preferences for activity sharing with friends and family.

Photo Privacy

If you use the Photos app on your watch:

- Open the "Settings" app on your watch.
- Scroll down and select "Photos."
- Adjust the settings for photo access and syncing with your iPhone.

In an age where data security and privacy concerns are on the rise, it's crucial to take proactive steps to protect your personal information. Apple Watch Series 8 offers a range of features and settings to help you achieve this goal. From setting up a strong passcode to managing app permissions and enabling privacy features, you have the tools to keep your data safe. By following the step-by-step guide outlined in this chapter, you can enjoy the convenience of your Apple Watch Series 8 while maintaining your privacy and security.

CHAPTER 9

EXPLORING FUTURE POSSIBILITIES

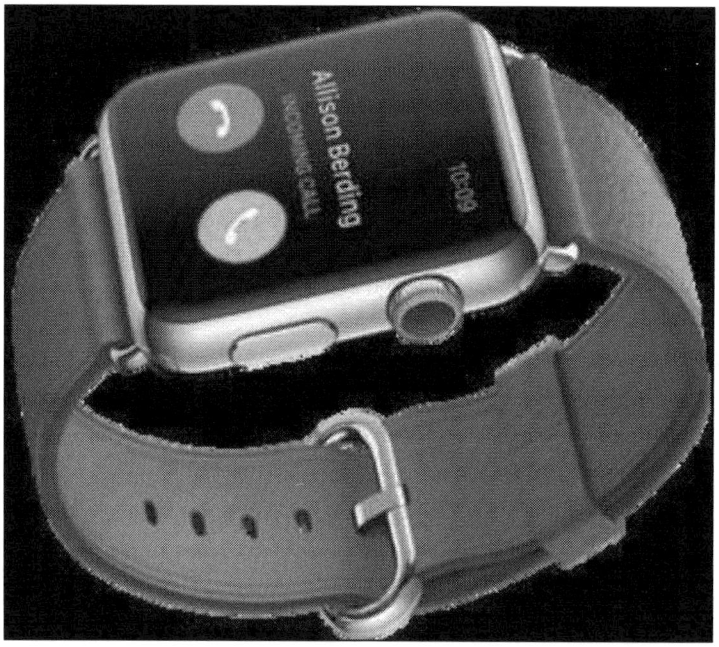

In the rapidly evolving landscape of wearable technology, the Apple Watch has emerged as a groundbreaking device, redefining our interactions with technology and health. The Apple Watch Series 8, in particular, stands at the forefront of innovation, showcasing a commitment to user-centric design and cutting-edge features. In Chapter 9 of the comprehensive guide, "Exploring Future Possibilities," we delve deep into the forthcoming features and updates of Series 8, with a specific focus on how seniors can seamlessly integrate wearables into their daily lives. Through this detailed exploration, we aim to shed light on the immense potential that wearable technology holds, especially for the senior demographic.

Upcoming Features and Updates: A Glimpse into the Future

The Apple Watch Series 8 is poised to introduce a host of exciting features and updates designed to cater to the unique needs and preferences of seniors. Apple's unwavering commitment to enhancing the user experience is evident in the meticulous attention given to seniors' distinct requirements, ensuring that the wearable device serves as an invaluable companion in their day-to-day lives. Let us delve into the significant upcoming features and updates that await users in the Series 8.

Enhanced Health and Wellness Monitoring

Health and wellness have always been a top priority for seniors, and the Apple Watch Series 8 aims to take monitoring to new heights. Equipped with an upgraded array of sensors and improved algorithms, seniors can expect more precise tracking of vital health metrics. From heart rate monitoring to detailed sleep analysis, the watch will provide invaluable insights to help users manage their health effectively. Moreover, the incorporation of features like fall detection and medication reminders underscores Apple's dedication to ensuring the safety and well-being of seniors, providing both individuals and their families with peace of mind.

Advanced Fitness Tracking and Customization

Staying active and maintaining a healthy lifestyle is paramount for seniors, and the Apple Watch Series 8 recognizes and addresses this need comprehensively. The upcoming iteration is expected to offer advanced fitness tracking capabilities, enabling users to monitor their workouts with unparalleled precision. With a wider range of exercise modes and the ability to set personalized fitness goals, seniors can tailor their fitness routines to suit their specific preferences and physical capabilities. Additionally, the option to customize workouts and receive real-time feedback will serve as a motivating factor, empowering users to achieve their fitness milestones and lead active, fulfilling lives.

Expanded Communication and Social Integration

Staying connected with loved ones is an essential aspect of a fulfilling life, especially for seniors. The Apple Watch Series 8 is set to introduce enhancements in communication features, making it more convenient and enjoyable to connect with family and friends. Anticipated improvements in messaging, voice calls, and video calls will facilitate seamless communication. Furthermore, the integration of social media platforms and streamlined notifications will ensure that seniors stay informed and engaged, reducing feelings of isolation and fostering a sense of community.

Augmented Reality (AR) and Virtual Reality (VR) Integration

Among the most exciting prospects for the Apple Watch Series 8 is the potential integration of augmented reality (AR) and virtual reality (VR) technologies. This forward-thinking approach will open up a world of interactive experiences and immersive learning opportunities for seniors. AR can aid in better navigation and understanding of their environment, making daily tasks more manageable. On the other hand, VR can transport users to virtual destinations, enhancing mental stimulation and engagement, which is particularly beneficial for seniors seeking mental enrichment and adventure within the confines of their homes.

Integrating Wearables into Daily Life: A Step-by-Step Guide

Understanding how to seamlessly integrate the Apple Watch Series 8 into daily life is vital for seniors to derive maximum benefits from this innovative device. Seniors, in particular, may require a step-by-step guide to familiarize themselves with the device and its capabilities effectively. Let us embark on a detailed journey through the process of incorporating the Series 8 into everyday routines, ensuring a smooth transition and optimal usage.

Familiarize Yourself with the Hardware and Software

To begin, it is imperative to gain a comprehensive understanding of the Apple Watch Series 8's hardware and software components. Take the time to learn about the physical attributes of the watch, such as the buttons, touchscreen controls, and how to navigate through its interface efficiently. Familiarize yourself with the pre-installed applications and explore the App Store to understand how to download new apps that cater to your interests and needs. Acquiring a foundational knowledge of the device's basics will set the stage for a more fluid integration process.

Customize Settings to Suit Your Preferences

Personalization plays a crucial role in making the Apple Watch Series 8 an extension of yourself. Dedicate time to customize settings according to your preferences and requirements. Begin by selecting and configuring watch faces that resonate with you, as this is often the first interaction you have with the device. Arrange app layouts to suit your usage patterns and prioritize apps that align with your daily activities. Adjust text size, display brightness, and font to ensure optimal visibility, particularly if you have specific visual needs. Tailoring the watch to your liking will significantly enhance user experience and make interactions more intuitive and enjoyable.

Set Up Health and Fitness Monitoring

The health and fitness features of the Apple Watch Series 8 are among its most powerful and transformative aspects. To leverage these capabilities effectively, start by setting up the health monitoring applications available on the device. Configure health-related preferences by inputting accurate personal data, such as age, weight, height, and any existing health conditions you

FAQ

1. What are the fundamental features of the Apple Watch Series 8?

The Apple Watch Series 8 is a versatile smartwatch that offers a range of features, including health and wellness monitoring, communication capabilities, productivity tools, and more. It's designed to enhance daily life and streamline various activities.

2. How can I navigate the Apple Watch Series 8 effectively?

Navigation on the Apple Watch Series 8 involves using the touch-sensitive screen, the Digital Crown, and gestures. Swiping, tapping, and rotating the Digital Crown allow you to access apps, notifications, and other functions seamlessly.

3. Can I customize the settings on the Apple Watch Series 8 to suit my preferences?

Yes, the Apple Watch Series 8 allows customization of various settings, such as watch faces, app arrangement, notification preferences, and more. This enables you to personalize your watch to align with your needs and preferences.

4. How can I interact with Siri on the Apple Watch Series 8?

You can interact with Siri on the Apple Watch Series 8 by raising your wrist and saying "Hey Siri" or by pressing and holding the Digital Crown. Siri can assist you with various tasks, answer questions, send messages, set reminders, and more.

5. How does the Apple Watch Series 8 monitor heart rate?

The Apple Watch Series 8 utilizes advanced sensors to monitor your heart rate throughout the day. It provides real-time data and can notify you of irregular heart rhythms, helping you maintain a better understanding of your cardiovascular health.

6. How does the Apple Watch Series 8 track physical activity?

The Apple Watch Series 8 has built-in accelerometers and gyroscopes to monitor your physical activities accurately. It tracks steps, distance, calories burned, and other metrics, allowing you to analyze your workouts and daily movement.

7. Can I manage my health data effectively using the Apple Watch Series 8?

Absolutely. The Apple Watch Series 8 allows you to store and manage various health-related data, such as medical records, allergies, medications, and more. This centralized management system aids in keeping your health information organized and accessible.

8. How can I make and receive calls on the Apple Watch Series 8?

You can make and receive calls directly on your Apple Watch Series 8 if it's connected to your iPhone. The watch acts as a speakerphone, allowing you to communicate without taking out your phone.

9. How can I send messages using the Apple Watch Series 8?

Sending messages on the Apple Watch Series 8 can be done through voice dictation, scribbling, using pre-set replies, or utilizing the on-screen keyboard. The watch seamlessly integrates with your iPhone's messaging apps for efficient communication.

10. How does Emergency SOS work on the Apple Watch Series 8?

In case of an emergency, pressing and holding the side button on the Apple Watch Series 8 will activate Emergency SOS. This feature can call emergency services and notify your emergency contacts with your current location.

11. How can I set reminders and alarms using the Apple Watch Series 8?

You can set reminders and alarms on the Apple Watch Series 8 through the built-in apps or third-party apps. Using your voice or the watch's interface, you can schedule reminders and alarms to help you stay organized and on track.

12. How can I use the Calendar feature on the Apple Watch Series 8?

The Calendar app on the Apple Watch Series 8 syncs with your iPhone's calendar, allowing you to view and manage your events and appointments directly from your wrist. You can also receive notifications for upcoming events.

13. How can I manage notifications on the Apple Watch Series 8?

Managing notifications on the Apple Watch Series 8 involves customizing which apps and types of notifications you receive. You can do this through the Watch app on your paired iPhone, tailoring the notifications to your preferences.

14. What are the advanced health monitoring features of the Apple Watch Series 8?

The Apple Watch Series 8 includes advanced health features such as ECG (Electrocardiogram) and blood oxygen monitoring. The ECG feature can detect irregular heart rhythms, while blood oxygen monitoring provides insights into your respiratory health.

15. How can I use third-party apps on the Apple Watch Series 8?

You can download and use third-party apps on the Apple Watch Series 8 through the Watch app on your iPhone. Once downloaded, these apps can be accessed and used directly on your watch, enhancing its functionality and versatility.

16. How can seniors create and track fitness goals using the Apple Watch Series 8?

Seniors can set fitness goals on the Apple Watch Series 8 using the Fitness app. Goals can range from step counts to calorie targets, providing motivation and a means to monitor progress towards a healthier lifestyle.

17. How does the Apple Watch Series 8 track sleep, and how can seniors benefit from this feature?

The Apple Watch Series 8 offers sleep-tracking capabilities, allowing seniors to monitor their sleep patterns and improve their sleep quality. This information can be valuable for maintaining overall well-being and addressing any sleep-related concerns.

18. How can seniors manage their medications using the Apple Watch Series 8?

Seniors can use the Health app on the Apple Watch Series 8 to set reminders for medications, ensuring they take them at the appropriate times. This feature helps seniors manage their health effectively and maintain a consistent medication schedule.

BONUS

TIPS FOR ADAPTING TO CHANGES IN WATCHOS

In the fast-paced world of technology, the Apple Watch Series 8 stands as a pinnacle of innovation, designed to seamlessly integrate into the lives of seniors, providing not just convenience but also health and safety features. However, with each new iteration of the WatchOS operating system, adapting to the changes and leveraging the full potential of this powerful wearable becomes increasingly crucial. This chapter, titled "Tips for Adapting to Changes in WatchOS," aims to equip seniors with essential insights and practical advice to navigate and make the most of the upgrades and new features in the Apple Watch Series 8.

Understanding WatchOS Evolution

The foundation of adapting to changes in WatchOS lies in comprehending its evolutionary journey. Over the years, Apple has continually refined and enhanced the WatchOS, integrating new features, improving user interface, and enhancing performance. The Apple Watch Series 8, the latest installment, represents the culmination of these efforts, promising a more intuitive and efficient user experience.

WatchOS 8: An Overview

The Apple Watch Series 8 comes pre-loaded with WatchOS 8, the latest version of the operating system. WatchOS 8 brings a host of new features and improvements, focusing on health and fitness, communication, and personalization. Understanding these features is essential for seniors to harness the full potential of their Apple Watch.

Health and Fitness Features

WatchOS 8 places a significant emphasis on health and fitness, offering features that are especially beneficial for seniors. One notable addition is the enhanced fall detection feature, which can automatically call emergency services if a fall is detected and the user is unresponsive. Moreover, WatchOS 8 introduces respiratory rate tracking, which provides valuable insights into overall well-being.

Communication Enhancements

For seniors, staying connected with loved ones is paramount. WatchOS 8 enhances communication capabilities by allowing users to share photos and messages directly from the watch, making it easier to stay in touch with family and friends. Additionally, updates to the Messages app streamline conversations and provide quicker access to essential functions.

Personalization and Accessibility

Personalizing the Apple Watch experience is vital to ensure it caters to individual needs and preferences. WatchOS 8 offers new watch faces, customizations, and the ability to add text to watch faces, enabling seniors to tailor their devices to their liking. Moreover, improved accessibility features enhance usability for seniors with varying abilities.

Tips for Adapting to WatchOS Changes

Adapting to changes in WatchOS requires a systematic approach, encompassing familiarization, utilization, and personalization. Seniors can optimize their Apple Watch Series 8 experience by following these essential tips:

Keep Abreast of Updates and Changes

Technology evolves rapidly, and so does WatchOS. Seniors must proactively seek out information regarding updates, new features, and changes introduced in each WatchOS version. Apple regularly publishes release notes and guides that provide valuable insights into what's new and how to utilize the latest features effectively.

Utilize Online Resources and Tutorials

The internet is a treasure trove of information and tutorials. Seniors should explore reputable online resources, Apple's official website, and video tutorials available on platforms like YouTube. These resources often offer step-by-step guides and demonstrations, making it easier to understand and implement the changes in WatchOS.

Engage in Hands-On Learning

The best way to learn and adapt is through hands-on experience. Seniors should dedicate time to exploring the Apple Watch and experimenting with the new features and functionalities introduced in WatchOS 8. By actively engaging with the device, they can familiarize themselves with the changes and gain a better understanding of how to incorporate them into their daily routines.

Leverage Apple Support and Customer Service

Apple provides exceptional customer support services, including online assistance and phone support. Seniors should not hesitate to reach out to Apple's support team to seek clarification or assistance in adapting to the changes in WatchOS. Apple support representatives are well-trained and can provide personalized guidance to address specific concerns.

Participate in Workshops and Community Events

Apple often organizes workshops and community events at Apple Stores or online. Seniors can benefit from attending these events to gain hands-on experience, learn from Apple experts, and interact with other users. Sharing experiences and insights with fellow seniors can foster a sense of community and encourage collaborative learning.

Establish a Routine for Learning and Practice

Consistency is key when adapting to changes. Seniors should establish a routine for dedicating time to learning and practicing new features. Setting aside a specific time each week for this purpose can help in gradually mastering the changes in WatchOS and ensuring a smooth transition.

Adapting to changes in technology, especially within the Apple Watch Series 8 and its evolving WatchOS, is a journey that demands patience, curiosity, and a proactive approach to learning. Seniors can navigate this journey successfully by staying informed, utilizing available resources, engaging in hands-on learning, seeking assistance when needed, and embracing a consistent learning routine. With these tips in mind, seniors can not only adapt to the changes in WatchOS but also unlock the full potential of their Apple Watch Series 8, enhancing their overall lifestyle and well-being.

CONCLUSION

After exploring the ins and outs of the Apple Watch Series 8, it's clear this impressive smartwatch offers immense value for seniors looking to enhance their lives through technology. By following the guidance in this book, you can fully capitalize on the Apple Watch's capabilities for health, communication, information, safety and much more.

A key takeaway is just how customizable the Apple Watch is to meet each senior's unique needs and preferences. Take the time to adjust settings for comfort and accessibility. Enable features like fall detection, Emergency SOS, and heart health notifications to provide peace of mind. Set up your favorite apps, contacts, news sources, and complications to get relevant info at a glance. There are so many options to create an Apple Watch experience that seamlessly integrates into your lifestyle.

While learning a new tech device takes time and patience, the instructions provided ensure you can progress at your own pace. Don't be afraid to experiment and explore – the intuitive design makes it hard to make catastrophic errors! If you do get stuck, there are troubleshooting tips for common issues. And you can always reset the watch to start fresh.

To get the most from your Apple Watch, make it a habit to interact with it daily. Keep tabs on your health data – it provides powerful insight to improve your well-being over time. Stay connected with loved ones through messages and calls. Use apps like Reminders, Calendar, and Timers to help you stay organized and punctual. Let the Apple Watch enhance your daily activities rather than completely change them.

This book guides you through the possibilities, but you determine how the Apple Watch ultimately impacts your life. Use it to pursue fitness goals that enable healthy aging. Maintain independence and confidence in your abilities. Stay current with technology and connected to your family and friends. The Apple Watch can provide as much or as little support in these areas as you desire.

While current features of the Series 8 are amazing, Apple Watch technology will only continue to advance. We can expect even more health sensors, smarter apps, and relevant notifications in the future. This book prepares you to easily adapt to new updates so you can continue benefiting from Apple Watch innovation for years to come.

I hope this guide has shown how accessible and life-enriching wearable technology can be for seniors. Approach your Apple Watch with an open mind and a sense of discovery. Don't be intimidated. With the knowledge you've gained, you are ready to maximize its potential in your life. So, embrace this opportunity to pursue an active, healthy, engaged lifestyle. The Apple Watch makes it easier than ever!

INDEX

Made in United States
Orlando, FL
10 November 2026

90510171R00037